WAR'S COST

WAR'S COST
The Hite's Civil War

DR. EUGENE DEFRIEST BÉTIT

Copyright © 2016 Dr. Eugene DeFriest Bétit
All rights reserved.

ISBN: 1530062713
ISBN 13: 9781530062713
Library of Congress Control Number: 2016902836
CreateSpace Independent Publishing Platform
North Charleston, South Carolina

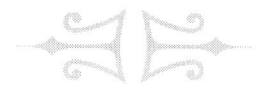

PREFACE

Although more than ten thousand books have already been written about the Civil War, hundreds more are published every year. Untapped sources—diaries and official records—as well as new research possibilities via the Internet have occasioned an explosion of new interpretations and an appreciation of this war, which pitted Americans against one another, often brother against brother, father against son.

Major Isaac Hite stemmed from a prosperous and prominent slave-owning family of the Shenandoah Valley. His industriousness facilitated the spectacular growth of Belle Grove Plantation, crowned by the construction of a magnificent manor home that enchants thousands of visitors each year. Headquarters to four Union commanders, the home is situated in the middle of Cedar Creek Battlefield, a lesser-known but critical battle that forever sealed the fate of the Confederacy in the Valley.

The Cost of War: The Hite Family in the Civil War exploits new sources to develop an in-depth study of one family's engagement in the war—and its consequences. Using The Virginia Regimental Histories Series, available data is marshaled for more than one hundred Hites who fought in the ranks of Virginia's units. Genealogical tools such as Ancestry.com and FindaGrave.com are used to provide fresh insights.

Gene Bétit
Winchester, Virginia, 2016

"Future years will never know the seething hell and the black infernal background, the countless minor scenes and interiors of the secession war; and it is best they should not. The real war will never get in the books."

-- WALT WHITMAN

"War is hell. It is only those who have neither fired a shot nor heard the shrieks and groans of the wounded who cry aloud for blood, more vengeance, more desolation."

-- GENERAL WILLIAM TECUMSEH SHERMAN

"It is well that war is so horrible, or we should get too fond of it."

-- GENERAL ROBERT E. LEE

CONTENTS

Preface ·v

Development of the Shenandoah Valley · · · · · · · · · · · · · · · · · · · 1
Education · 6
Slavery · 10
Conditions in the Valley · 17
Intermarriage with the First Families of Virginia · · · · · · · · · · · · · · · · · 22
Hite Participation in the Civil War · 23
"Last Full Measure" · 29
The Survivors · 39
War's Aftermath · 50

Endnotes · 55
Bibliography · 64
Appendix A · 68
Appendix B · 84
Appendix C ·107
Appendix D ·118
Index ·122

GRAPHICS

Belle Grove at sunrise, National Park Service volunteer Buddy Secor, Cedar Creek and Belle Grove National Historic Park 2
Charles Peale Polk, *Portrait of Major Isaac Hite Jr.*, oil on canvas, 60 × 42 inches, 1799. Belle Grove Plantation Collection, Middletown, Frederick County, Virginia 3
Occupations of Winchester, Lewis N. Barton, Winchester-Frederick County Historical Society, Volume 3, p. 9-13 21
Hite Participants by Side and State 24
Samuel C. Hite, tombstone, Andersonville, Georgia, FindaGrave.com ... 26
Geographical Disposition of Hite Fatalities, courtesy Charles E. Brewer 29
Area of Operations, Army of Northern Virginia 32
The Terror of War, Harpers Weekly, date unknown 34
Cavalry Melee at Brandy Station, drawing by Edwin Forbes, 1864, Library of Congress Prints and Photographs Division Collection, Washington, DC 38
Dr. Robert Stuart Baldwin, ambrotype, Ancestry.com 39
Isaac Bird Hite, ambrotype, Heuvel, *Remembering Virginia's Confederates* 41
Cornelius Baldwin Hite/Archibald Magill, ambrotypes, 1st and 6th Virginia Cavalry regimental histories 42

William Smith Davison, ambrotype, Ancestry.com · · · · · · · · · · · · · · · ·47
William Smith Davison, artifacts from his oldest daughter
Edmonia, http://cinderspark.com/family/annawilliam.html · · · · · · · · · · 48
William Smith Davison, tombstone, FindaGrave.com · · · · · · · · · · · · · · · ·49
"Wood" Hite and Frank and Jesse James posters, FindaGrave.com · · · · · ·51
David Christian Hite, ambrotype and memorial, *The Painful News* · · · · · ·70
John C. Hite's tombstone and cemetery record, correspondence with
administrative and accounting manager for Old City Cemetery,
Lynchburg, Virginia, July 27, 2015, and
www.gravegarden.org/diuguid/details.php? id=SB0112906· · · · · · · · · · · · ·73
John M. Hite tombstones, FindaGrave.com ·75
John Pendleton Hite, ambrotype, Ancestry.com and headstone
in Hollywood Cemetery, Richmond. ·76
John Pendleton Hite memorial notice, *The Painful News* · · · · · · · · · · · · 77
Thomas G. Hite, tombstone, FindaGrave.com· 80
Isaac Martin Hite, ambrotype, Ancestry.com· ·93

FIGURES

Figure 1. Southside Racial Composition· ·12
Figure 2. Slave Population in the South ·14
Figure 3. 1834 Slave Population of Frederick County· · · · · · · · · · · · · · · ·18
Figure 4. Major Hite's Grandsons' Participation in the Civil War · · · · · · ·23
Figure 5. Hite Participation by Side and State ·24

APPENDICES

A. Virginia Hites Who Died Fighting for the Confederacy · · · · · · · · · · · 68
B. The Survivors · 84
C. Ancestry.com Roster of Civil War Hites · 107
D. Major Hite's Grandsons · 118

DEVELOPMENT OF THE SHENANDOAH VALLEY

Major Isaac Hite Jr. (1758–1836), a prosperous Shenandoah Valley farmer and entrepreneurial businessman who achieved national recognition for progressive and productive agricultural techniques, constructed Belle Grove Plantation* near Middletown in Frederick County, Virginia, between 1794 and 1797. This stately country manor home's design had direct architectural input from Thomas Jefferson. It is substantially built, with two-foot-thick walls of locally quarried limestone. Belle Grove Plantation witnessed the conversion of the Valley wilderness into a thriving breadbasket and was the site of one of the most decisive battles of the Civil War.

---

* The Hite family sold Belle Grove in 1860. Although the house was headquarters for four federal commanders during the Civil War, and the battle of Cedar Creek raged around it on October 19, 1864, it emerged essentially unscathed. One of twenty-seven historical sites of the National Trust for Historic Preservation, Belle Grove today is furnished much as it was in the early 1800s and includes the manor home, original icehouse and smokehouse, a slave cemetery, a heritage apple orchard, demonstration colonial garden, and an early twentieth-century barn. Belle Grove is part of the 3,700-acre Cedar Creek and Belle Grove National Historical Park, a partnership park established in 2002, which includes the National Park Service, four nonprofit organizations, and Shenandoah County.

Belle Grove (Middletown, Virginia) at sunrise

Isaac was the grandson of Jost Hite (Hans Justus Heyd), among the first European settlers who settled the Shenandoah Valley. Born in Bonfeld, about forty miles southeast of Heidelberg, Germany, in December 1685, Jost and his family left Europe to avoid the religious wars that wracked Europe for more than a century. Millions perished in the Thirty Years' War (1618–1648) alone; in addition, both sides were involved in periodic religious massacres for nearly two hundred years. In 1710, Jost emigrated under English indenture to Kingston, New York, but soon relocated to Germantown, near Philadelphia, Pennsylvania, where he prospered. In 1729, Hite learned that the colonial governor of Virginia was offering huge land tracts to encourage settlement of the wilderness lands west of the Blue Ridge Mountains. Between 1730 and 1732, Governors William Gooch and Alexander Spottswood of Virginia ratified nine large land grants totaling 385,000 acres west of the Blue Ridge Mountains to individuals who agreed to settle Virginia's virgin Shenandoah Valley, part of a plan to create a buffer to secure the area from French and Indian incursions. In 1732, Jost was granted 100,000 acres on the condition that he settle one hundred families in the Valley. He sold his extensive holdings, now known as Pennypacker Mills,** near Germantown, outside of Philadelphia, and relocated with sixteen other families into the then trackless frontier to an area just south of Winchester that same year. This group, some one hundred individuals, had to first clear a path for wagons along the Great Indian Trail. Creating a wagon road out of a path from Pennsylvania to the Opequon River near Winchester likely required several months. Other parties participated in the settlement of the Valley, notably Scotsman Alexander Ross, whose seventy-family Quaker community located ten miles to the northeast.

Major Isaac Hite Jr.

Development of the Shenandoah Valley was relatively swift. Orange County was formed in 1734; it was divided in 1738, with Frederick and

---

** His Pennsylvania holdings were purchased in 1747 by Peter Pennypacker and became home to eight generations of that family, including Pennsylvania's twenty-third governor, Samuel W. Pennypacker. Hite's mansion, built around 1720, was used as headquarters by George Washington during the battle of Germantown in 1777. Belle Grove, Pennypacker Mills, and Springdale are enrolled in the National Register of Historic Places.

DEVELOPMENT OF THE SHENANDOAH VALLEY

Augusta Counties created in the territory west of the "Great Mountains" (Blue Ridge). Jost served as a local magistrate in Frederick County, along with Lord Thomas Fairfax, who had come to the frontier to supervise administration of his five-million-acre Northern Neck Proprietary (inherited from King Charles II's huge grant made in 1649).

Jost and most of his family owned slaves. Jost's oldest son, Colonel John Hite, was appointed county lieutenant to replace Lord Fairfax. John was a large-scale slave-owner who built a large limestone house, Springdale, in what is now Stephens City, just south of Winchester in 1753. However, the land the House of Burgesses and Virginia's governors deeded to Jost Hite and others fell within territory belonging to Lord Fairfax, and Jost and Lord Fairfax were soon engaged in a protracted (1749–1802) court suit that was resolved only after the Revolution and the death of both parties. Although it was settled in Hite's favor, Lord Fairfax, the sole English peer who came to the New World, elected to remain in America and is buried in the courtyard of Christ Episcopal Church in Winchester.

By 1800, some 999 land grants had been issued in the lower Shenandoah Valley, with immigrants arriving principally from Pennsylvania, New Jersey, and New York. In contrast with the original settlers of Virginia, these newcomers were in the main neither English nor members of the Church of England. They brought cultures into the Valley that differed markedly from the predominant lifestyle of the Tidewater planters who settled the rest of Virginia. Most were small-scale farmers and included many Mennonites and Church of the Brethren members.

Jost's great-grandson, Isaac Hite Jr., received his education at the College of William and Mary, where he was secretary of the Phi Beta Kappa Fraternity. When the college closed during the Revolutionary War, Isaac enlisted in the Continental army, serving as aide to General Peter Muhlenberg, who commanded one of Virginia's divisions. Isaac was present at the British surrender at Yorktown and inventoried the weapons surrendered by the British. In

1783, he married Eleanor "Nelly" Madison, President James Madison's sister, and returned to Middletown. With the 483 acres his father gave him as a wedding present and Colonel James Madison Sr.'s gift of fifteen slaves, Isaac built a prosperous enterprise, expanding to a 7,500-acre plantation, cultivating grain and livestock with several grain and lumber mills, a general store, and distillery. In recognition of his prominence and military experience, he was commissioned a militia major by Governor Patrick Henry. As mentioned, Isaac built Belle Grove between 1794 and 1797, but even before its completion, he was visited by his brother-in-law, then-Congressman James Madison, and his new wife, the twenty-six-year-old widow Dolley Payne Todd, during their honeymoon in the fall of 1794. Strategically located on the Valley Pike, the major immigration trail for wagon trains of "land schooners"—Conestoga wagons—thousands of pioneers passed by Belle Grove bound for Kentucky, Tennessee, Ohio, and points south.

Unfortunately, Nelly died of pneumonia the day before Christmas in 1802, and only two of their three children grew to adulthood. A year after Eleanor's death, Major Hite married Ann Tunstall Maury, a woman who was twenty years younger than he, who bore him ten children, all of whom survived to adulthood.

Major Hite's family's support for the Southern cause is typical of other Valley families' experience, and the effect of their service is a microcosm of the calamitous effect the Civil War had on the entire US population. Nearly all of the Shenandoah Valley's Hites of military age enlisted, with at least one hundred Hites from Virginia serving as privates. One Hite enlisted as a lieutenant and two others were promoted to lieutenant during the course of the war, while several were promoted to the noncommissioned officer ranks. This is rather remarkable, considering the fact that Isaac was a militia major, his uncle John was a militia colonel, and the family included a significant number of captains, majors, and colonels before the Civil War. Furthermore, several in-laws were generals. A likely cause for this dramatic shift within two generations is lack of education.

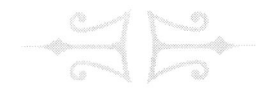

EDUCATION

Public education did not exist in Winchester, the Shenandoah Valley, or throughout the state of Virginia generally until 1870. Naturally, this lack of education, which extended throughout the South, was reflected in high illiteracy rates.[1] Before 1870, all education in Winchester and throughout the state was provided by small private schools, many of which existed only a few years. A recent study found that from the eighteenth century until the establishment of public education in 1870, there were more than fifty private schools in Winchester and at least as many more in Frederick County.[2] Parents were expected to arrange and pay for their children's education in the prewar era.[3] Wealthy families usually hired tutors or governesses, so that education was commonly available only for the "First Families of Virginia." The *Richmond Examiner* proclaimed in 1856 that "free schools are of the same brood of damnableness whose mother is sin and whose daddy is the devil."[4] Historian Charles S. Sydnor, confirming that there was no systematic school system in Virginia at this time, noted that such schools as did exist were in log cabins, in which all classes were taught by a single teacher, as often as not by a minister. Sydnor has noted that in consequence, "a cloud of ignorance laid heavy over much of the South."[5] Large landowners evidently feared that education would empower the laboring classes; education of slaves was strictly forbidden.

Early in the eighteenth century an ongoing struggle between church and state also contributed to the reluctance to provide public education—each denomination was concerned that public education would impinge on their religious prerogatives. Even Thomas Jefferson saw education as generally "operating in the interest of the church rather than the state."[6]

J. E. Norris, a late-nineteenth-century historian, noted that aside from private education, "charity" schools existed, "sometimes kept at the expense of the city or town…and sometimes through the generosity of an individual… none but extremely poor parents ever thought of sending their children to them." He noted that they were "patronized mostly by orphans or very indigent persons." For this reason, he wrote, "there was a certain stigma attached to these lower schools, not alone from the contact with poor children, whose rude manners may have been entailed upon them by a drunken father or worthless mother, but from the innate Virginian idea of independence." Norris asserted that when a free school system was suggested, it was met with bitter opposition on the part of a large majority of the citizens of the commonwealth.[7] No doubt this paternalistic attitude prevailed among the ruling class, but its contempt for the average citizen is apparent. Unfortunately, insistence on maintaining control at all costs contributed to Virginia's loss of national stature, power, and reputation. It also had unintended and lasting consequences.

This attitude applied even to higher education; Sydnor observed that "all of the Southern colleges were allied either with church or state in 1820; the church colleges, with the exception of Georgetown founded by the Catholics in 1815, were under either Presbyterian or Episcopalian influence."[8]

As renowned historian James M. McPherson has noted, one of Reconstruction's proudest achievements was establishing a public school system for both races throughout the South. Virginia did not provide statewide public education until the Underwood Constitution in 1870, passed by the Republican-controlled General Assembly during the Reconstruction period.

However, once they were rid of the despised "carpetbaggers" (generally, men who came south to invest and help the South get back on its feet) and "scallywags" (loyal Unionists), Virginia's conservative legislators restricted the funding available for education. The traditional power structure, the large plantation owners, industrialists, and wealthy bankers, still considered universal education a "Yankee error" and continued to believe that parents should be responsible for ensuring that their offspring received an education.[9] Under the guise of a conservative "pay-as-you-go" fiscal policy, the resurgent prewar power structure endeavored to preserve the former patriarchal system and deny both poor whites and blacks education and wider economic opportunity.

In 1880, 20 percent of whites and over 70 percent of blacks were still illiterate. Less than 60 percent of white children and 40 percent of black children of school age attended school, and the average school term was three months or less.[10] When the 1880 census determined that over six million Americans aged ten and over could not read and write, Senator Henry W. Blair of New Hampshire introduced a bill that would have appropriated $77 million (some $700 million in 1981 values) over seven years for public schools, to be distributed based on illiteracy rates. However, The Democrats' opposition in the House repeatedly defeated the measure because of concerns over states' rights, fear that it might end up being a means to restore Reconstruction, and a desire to maintain lower taxes.[11]

As late as 1900, less than half of Virginia's school-age population was attending school, and there was only one public high school in the entire state. In June 1902, as part of Jim Crow, a General Assembly convention finally replaced the despised Underwood Constitution, disenfranchising nearly all of the black and about half of the white electorate. Virginia's Mann High School Bill, passed in 1906 after a close vote in the General Assembly, authorized modest funds for high school programs, but localities had to furnish adequate buildings and pay teachers' salaries. During the 1920s, Virginia's per capita spending was four times as much on white pupils as it was for black students and there were only eight four-year full-time black high schools in the state compared to about four hundred white high schools.[12] The illiteracy rate was still 11 percent for whites; 45 percent of blacks were illiterate in the 1920s.[13]

For the Hites in particular and the South in general, it is unfortunate that education was not generally available. The Hite family's experience is clear evidence that lack of education came at a considerable cost in undeveloped potential and personal capability.

SLAVERY

Slave traders

Chattel slavery originally existed in all thirteen colonies, although it had all but disappeared north of the Mason-Dixon Line by 1860. As is well known, the antebellum Southern economy was heavily dependent on slave labor, and fear of insurrection, as exemplified in the uprisings in Haiti from 1791 to 1804, lurked constantly in every Southerner's mind. As Henry Tragle noted in *The Southampton Slave Revolt of 1831*, after Nat Turner's Rebellion that year, Virginia became "an armed and garrisoned state." With a total population of 1,211,405, the state of Virginia fielded a "militia force of 101,488 men, including cavalry, artillery, grenadiers, riflemen, and light infantry."[14] Tragle observed that this was at a time when Virginia faced no exterior threat. Nevertheless, the state maintained a military force equal to 10 percent of its total population, including both black and white inhabitants.

In the decade preceding the Civil War, relations with the North, where slavery gradually was becoming less prevalent, and the South, which increasingly depended on its "peculiar institution" to drive its agrarian economy, were progressively aggravated. John Brown's attack on the federal armory at Harpers Ferry to liberate slaves on October 16, 1859, heightened tensions to such an extent that prominent men began raising additional military units and conducting regular militia drills. Militia units drilled more frequently and with greater seriousness. Brown's raid struck a chord in the perpetual fear of white Southerners that the Negro population would rise in rebellion. The *Richmond Enquirer* asserted that the raid on Harpers Ferry "advanced the cause of disunion more than any other event."[15] The early enlistment dates that we will see for many individuals reflect the fact that many units, both militia and those formed in a reaction to Brown's action, were activated once the Ordinance of Secession was ratified, and in some cases, even in advance.

Further, Richard Duncan notes that the generation born between 1830 and 1842 was extremely critical of the region's decline under their elders.[16] The younger generation generally saw secession as a moral cleansing of Virginia and the South from the aggressive, abolitionist-led North. Above all, the triumph of the "Black Republicans" in the election of 1860 was seen as an insult to Southerners, resulting in a widespread sense of dishonor and inferiority, and presenting a clear threat to property, prosperity and the Southern economy and way of life.[17] One exasperated father wrote to the Virginia Military Institute's Colonel Francis W. Smith: "The military fever is so rife among our young men that parents are sorely put to know how to restrain or govern their sons."[18]

In Virginia, the fervor, in some cases frenzy, of the populace for war varied from county to county. In Shenandoah County, 2,513 individuals voted to elect delegates to the secession congress after Fort Sumter was fired upon when Lincoln called for each state to provide troops to put down the rebellion. Only 5 voted against secession.[19] It should be noted that voting was done by open ballot at the time, so each man's vote was public knowledge. Most likely, feeling nowhere ran higher than in Southside, the area south of the James River, which was heavily dependent on slave labor. Here the percentage of the slave population often exceeded the white population, and there was a very large contingent of "fire-eaters," men who had decided that the time for discussion was over and who were ready and eager to join their cousins in the Cotton States of the Deep South in secession, even before Fort Sumter had been fired upon. The *Richmond Enquirer* reported that a convention in Lunenburg County on March 11, 1861, declared,

County	Whites	Percentage	Free Blacks	Percentage	Slaves	Percentage	Total
Brunswick	4,993	33.7	630	4.5	9,148	61.8	14,811
Buckingham	6,041	39.7	360	2.4	8,811	57.9	15,212
Halifax	11,066	41.7	558	2.1	14,897	56.2	26,521
Henrico	37,984	61.7	3,591	5.8	20,041	32.5	61,616
Lunenburg	4,447	37.1	232	1.9	7,305	61.0	11,984
Powhatan	2,589	34.1	399	4.8	5403	64.4	8,391
Prince Edward	4,038	34.1	465	3.9	7,341	62.0	11,844
Total	71,158	47.3	6,274	4.2	73,036	48.5	150,469

Figure 1: Southside Racial Composition[21]

"(We)...desire to leave...the dishonored ruins to the care of those who wantonly undermined its once grand and lofty pillars. (We) are eager to detach the old 'mother of states and statesmen' from the accursed North, ere (before) its fierce and desolating tide of furious fanaticism shall sweep ere (previously) hallowed soil."[20] Before and during the presidential election of 1860, rising militancy and a gradual slide toward armed conflict existed in the North as well, reflected particularly in the 'Wide Awakes,' a paramilitary organization affiliated with the Republican Party. Similar organizations affiliated with the Democratic Party were called 'Douglas Invincibles,' 'Young Hickories,' or 'Earthquakes.'"[22]

To understand the fervor and determination that sustained Southerners throughout four years of bitter conflict, one must appreciate how critical slavery was to the Southern economy. Thomas A. Ashby (1848–1916) expressed the sentiment of the majority of Virginia's citizens when he wrote, "To the people of my generation in the South, the ownership of slaves was an inheritance representing an investment (of millions of dollars), a property interest as necessary and valuable to its possessor as bonds and stocks."[23] Overall, the number of blacks was nearly half as large as the white population, although proportions varied widely from state to state.

State	White Population	Slave Population
	Lower South	
Alabama	519,121	435,080
Florida	78,679	61,745
Georgia	505,088	462,198
Louisiana	376,276	331,726
Mississippi	354,674	436,631
South Carolina	301,302	402,406
Texas	421,649	182,566
TOTAL	2,556,789	2,312,352

	Upper South	
Arkansas	324,335	111,115
North Carolina	661,563	331,099
Tennessee	834,082	275,719
Virginia	1,105,453	490,865
TOTAL	2,925,433	1,208,798

Figure 2: Slave Population in the South
Source: Wikipedia.com

Ashby probably expressed prevailing attitudes when he opined "the ownership of slaves involved, as a general rule, as little discomfort as the ownership of domestic animals." Obviously, while most slave owners might have convinced themselves that this was true, most slaves certainly did not think of themselves as pets. The numbers of "runaways" who risked capture by slave patrols and the ensuing consequences to escape north via the Underground Railroad provides evidence that this is so.

Ashby noted that he often played and "romped" with the young Negroes his age and worked with them in "easy duties" around the home. Most Southern whites' paternalistic attitude is reflected in another of Ashby's observations: "In his natural temperament the Negro is usually a happy, indolent, and frivolous character, fond of his ease, pleasures, and appetites." Elsewhere he observed, "His hardships were usually of his own making, brought on by vice and intemperance." Ashby reflected the South's irritation with the abolitionist viewpoint when he observed, "People who viewed slavery from a distance, who knew but little of its humane and civilizing influences over the Negro race, took isolated and unusual examples for universal conditions." He insisted that slaves were owned by the "wealthiest and best people," motivated by "guardianship and responsibility."[24]

By the time of the Civil War, the nearly four million slaves in the United States, predominantly in the South, had an approximate market value of close to four billion dollars, a large component of the gross national wealth.[25] Slave masters enjoyed rates of return on slaves significantly greater than those on other investments. Cotton consumers, insurance companies, and industrial enterprises alike benefited from slavery, and in general the entire Southern economy, in particular cotton, rice, and tobacco cultivation, was built on this "peculiar institution." Northern cotton mills and New York financial system were also indirectly dependent on human chattel. Such valuable "property" required rules to protect it, and the institutional practices and codes surrounding slavery displayed a sophistication that rivals present-day corporate law and business regulation.[26]

The institution of slavery steadily declined in the Valley for three decades before 1860. However, there was still widespread seasonal rental of slave labor, particularly for planting and harvesting. Free Blacks even hired out their own children.[27] Although nearly every religious denomination in the Valley opposed slavery, slaves still comprised nearly 20 percent of the Shenandoah Valley's population. The concentration of slaves throughout the Valley varied, but was notably higher in Clarke and Jefferson Counties, which had roots in the Tidewater planter culture.[28] As has been mentioned, the Shenandoah Valley's ethnic composition differed significantly from the rest of the state. The Valley had been settled predominantly by pioneers who came from Pennsylvania, New Jersey, New York, or directly from Europe. With the exception of Clarke and Jefferson Counties, settled by descendants of planters from the Tidewater region, there were very few large plantations in the Shenandoah Valley with large numbers of slaves.[29]

In 1860, the population of Shenandoah County stood at 13,896, including 753 slaves.[30] However, only 466 slaves were between the primary working age of twelve and sixty-five.[31] The black population of the county had reached its zenith in 1830 when there were 2,423 slaves in the county.[32] The reasons for the decline are not clear, but neighboring counties' patterns also followed this trend. No doubt the national depression of 1820 was a factor. The relatively small but highly productive farms in the Valley did not lend themselves to this "peculiar institution" as well as did the large plantations in the Deep South.[33] Belle Grove experienced its highest slave population of around 103 in 1815. Whatever the reason, many slaves from the Valley began to be sold southward.

In 1824, Major Hite advertised the sale of sixty slaves.[34] The 1850 census's slave schedule for Frederick County indicates that Major Hite's widow, Ann Maury Hite, owned sixteen slaves, while her sons Isaac Fontaine Hite Sr. owned sixteen, Walker Maury Hite Sr. owned fifteen, and Hugh Holmes Hite Sr. had five.[35] Slaves, like land and other property, were willed to children or gifted as they came of age, another factor that reduced the number of slaves on individual farms over time.

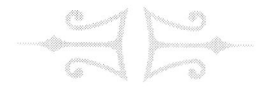

CONDITIONS IN THE VALLEY

A number of foreign visitors made a point of visiting the Shenandoah Valley in the years just before and after the Revolutionary War. Andrew Burnaby journeyed to the lower Valley, the area around Winchester, in 1760 and observed with regard to the inhabitants that "if there was such a thing as happiness in this life, they enjoy it…They are ignorant of want, and…possess what many princes would give half their dominions for, health, content and tranquility of mind."[36] Ferdinand Bayard, escaping the danger of the French Revolution in 1791, called the Valley a "promised land, from whose bosom is arising an innumerable population of well-to-do and happy men." He foresaw that these hardy people would expand, "passing soon beyond the confines of the valley, will overflow all the surrounding country and will make a vast wilderness productive."[37]

Isaac Weld, a Dubliner who visited the Shenandoah Valley in the late 1790s, noted, "The cultivated lands in this country are mostly parceled out in small sections. There are no persons here, as on the other side of the mountains, possessing large farms, nor are there those eminently distinguished by their education and knowledge from their fellow citizens. Poverty is as much unknown in this country as is great wealth…Everyone appears to be in a happy state of mediocrity and unambitious for more."[37]

As with many travelers, Weld did not notice everything. None of the three travelers, in fact, appears to have noticed and certainly did not record that in 1790 one in seven Valley residents was a slave. In Clarke and Jefferson counties the proportion reached one in four by the end of the century. Indeed, a considerable divide had developed between the eastern part of Frederick county settled by planters from the Tidewater region and the predominantly German and Scotch-Irish farmers and merchants who emigrated from Pennsylvania and points north, settling the western half. Between 1830 and 1840, the number of slaves in the area along the Shenandoah River, which would become Clarke county, increased, while in that same decade the slave population declined by a third in present-day Frederick County.[38] By the 1830s, disparity in wealth and population had become so pronounced that the slaveholders of eastern Frederick petitioned for the creation of a separate county.[39]

Their petition of December 4, 1834, provided a tabulation of the 1830 census population divided into two sections. "Eastern Frederick" included what would later become parts of Warren as well as Clarke County.[40]

	Freemen	Slaves	Aggregate
Eastern Frederick	8,706	5,332	14,100
Western Frederick	9,808	2,098	11,946

Figure 3: 1834 Slave Population of Frederick County

Winchester's economic decline was due in part to inadequate transportation. Political obstacles hampered funding for infrastructure improvement, and by 1831, three competing schemes had emerged. Major Hite's oldest son, James Madison Hite Sr., spearheaded an initiative to build a canal along the Shenandoah River from his plantation, Guilford, in what is now Clarke

County.[41] This was strongly opposed by the smaller farmers to the west, who advocated a turnpike down the center of the Valley to Harpers Ferry, where it would tie into the Baltimore and Ohio Railroad and the Chesapeake and Ohio Canal. Instead, in March 1831, the Virginia General Assembly approved construction of the Northwestern Turnpike from Winchester to Parkersburg on the Ohio River in present-day West Virginia. It was completed in 1838, and is the approximate route of today's US 50.

The Valley Pike, linking Winchester with Harrisonburg, was finished soon after, built largely by private investment, resulting in an endless series of toll collectors. It would eventually extend as far south as Staunton, was macadamized, and was a major factor during the Civil War.[42] Only later were good roads extended to the east into Clarke County, inhabited by the planter minority. The third competing proposal was construction of a rail line from Winchester to Harpers Ferry, which seems to have gained the most enthusiasm. The Winchester and Potomac spur was opened in 1836, but the line was not as well-built as more important main-line links.

According to the census of 1840, 80 percent of Virginians worked on farms, but by the 1850 census, only 48 percent of Virginia's free male population were classified as farmers or planters, with about 20 percent listed as laborers.[43] Like most of their neighbors, many Hites were farmers, consistent with the time and the family's heritage. Some were listed as "farm hands" or laborers—probably sons working on their fathers' farms.

In the years leading up to the Civil War, the Shenandoah Valley was widely known as the breadbasket of the South. Shenandoah County produced roughly three times as much grain (wheat, corn, rye, and barley) per capita as the other areas of the state. In the decade from 1790 to 1800, Frederick County, which as noted included areas of what subsequently became Clarke and Warren Counties, grew by more than 3,000 to a total population of 24,500.[44]

CONDITIONS IN THE VALLEY

By the eve of the Civil War, Winchester's regional predominance had slipped somewhat, challenged by Martinsburg twenty miles to the north and Staunton ninety miles south. The Chesapeake & Ohio Canal and Baltimore & Ohio Railroad had opened western trade and bypassed the town. By 1860, Frederick County had roughly 16,500 inhabitants, of which 2,300 were slaves; countywide, only 405 households owned slaves and only three households owned more than 20 slaves.[45] Winchester, a prosperous market town and the county seat, had a population of 4,400, with about three thousand whites in 701 households. There were 708 slaves and 680 free blacks; these 1,363 blacks made up nearly a third of the town's population. Less than a fifth of townspeople and county residents owned slaves—slaves made up only 13.7 percent of the total population.[46] There were two newspapers, several banks, over fifty stores, twelve churches, one large hotel (the Taylor), and a number of taverns. The streets were paved and gaslight had been introduced in 1855. A new medical college had recently been established.

The Valley's demonstrated fertility made it a strategic region for both sides during the four years of the Civil War. Winchester, an important market center, was served by a network of well-developed roads that radiated in nine directions. Its proximity to the Chesapeake & Ohio Canal and the Baltimore & Ohio Railroad made it an important strategic objective for both armies. Although tactically and strategically important, the surrounding terrain made the town indefensible. For these reasons, nearly as many battles and skirmishes were fought in the Shenandoah Valley during the four years of the war as in the rest of Virginia. The National Park Service estimates that 365 significant actions took place in the Valley—combat of some kind every four days.

OCCUPATIONS OF WINCHESTER

Period	Status	Commander
March 12–May 25, 1862	Federal	Banks
May 25–May 31, 1862	Confederate	Jackson
May 31–June 3, 1862	Between the Lines	
June 4–Sept. 2, 1862	Federal	Sigel
Sept. 3–Nov. 21, 1862	Confederate	Jackson
Nov. 22–Dec. 13, 1862*	Confederate	Jones
Dec. 14–Dec. 23, 1862	Between the Lines	
Dec. 24–June 13, 1863	Federal	Milroy
June 14–July 23, 1863	Confederate	Ewell et al.
July 24–Apr. 31, 1864	Between the Lines	
May 1–July 1, 1864	Federal	Sigel
July 2–July 20, 1864	Confederate	Early
July 21–July 24, 1864	Federal	Averill and Crook
July 24–Aug. 11, 1864	Confederate	Early
Aug. 11–Aug. 17, 1864	Federal	Sheridan
Aug. 17–Sept. 19, 1864	Confederate	Early
Sept. 19–April 9, 1865	Federal	Sheridan et al.

* Dec. 5, 1862, Gen. Geary occupied the town for two hours.

	Confederate Control No. of Days %		Between the Lines No. of Days %		Federal Occupation No. of Days %	
1861 (a)	265	100%	—	100%	—	—
1862	177	48	13	4	175	48%
1863	31	9	162	44	172	47
1864	96	26	121	33	148	41
1865 (b)	—	—	—	—	99	100
TOTAL	569	39%	296	20%	594	41%

(a) From April 10. (b) Thru April 9.

The information in this chart is derived largely from the diary of Julia Chase, as outlined by Lewis N. Barton in *W.–F.C.H.S. Papers*, Vol. 3, pp. 9–13.

Historians generally note that Winchester changed hands more than seventy times, a somewhat misleading figure because this figure includes frequent cavalry incursions not resulting in permanent change of control. Occupation of the town changed hands thirteen times, and Winchester endured seven federal occupations.[47]

INTERMARRIAGE WITH THE FIRST FAMILIES OF VIRGINIA

Prior to the Civil War, Major Hite's offspring and the wider Hite family married into numerous prominent Virginia families who were part of the aristocratic core of Virginia, dominating the state's political and economic structure for centuries. Isaac's offspring married into the Beale, Byrd, Clark (Revolutionary War General Jonathan Clark and William Clark, Corps of Discovery, which opened up the West), Davison, Fontaine, Lee, Madison, Marshall, Maury, Meade, Randolph, Rutherford, Smith, Taylor, Walker, Williams, and other families. By the fourth generation following Jost Hite's immigration into the Valley, Major Hite's grandsons had grown up with second and third cousins from these and other extended prominent families, including the most elite First Families of Virginia, and traveled in the same social circles. They were completely imbued with the Southern way of life and culture. The motivation for the Hites' service in the Confederate army is clear; it is not surprising that they rose to a man to defend the Southern way of life and values. Major Hite would have been proud of their dedication and loyalty, but as we will see, the cost was extremely high. It is also tragic that four generations after fleeing Europe's religious persecution, Hites participated on both sides of our fratricidal, bitter, and titanic war.

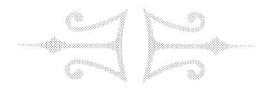

HITE PARTICIPATION IN THE CIVIL WAR

Major Hite had forty grandsons, not all of whom fought in the Civil War. Four of Major Hite's grandsons gave their lives for the Confederacy and two great-grandsons died for the cause. In addition, twenty-two Hites from other branches of the family died supporting the Confederacy (appendix A, p.68). Nine more grandsons and a great-grandson who lost his right arm enlisted, fought, and survived the war, as well as at least fifty-one other Hites from Virginia (appendix B, p 84).

Killed in Action	Served in CSA, Survived	Eligible, Did Not Serve	Too Old	Too Young	Dead before the War	Insufficient Information	TOTAL
4	9	2	6	10	8	1	40

Figure 4: Major Hite's Grandsons' Participation in the Civil War
Source: Author's analysis of Ancestry.com data
(See appendix D, p. 118, for details on each descendant.)

HITE PARTICIPATION IN THE CIVIL WAR

As we will see, large numbers of Hites from Virginia enlisted in the Southern cause. *The Roster of Confederate Soldiers, 1861–1865, Volume VIII,* lists one hundred two Hites from Virginia, including fourteen enrolled in local militia units. Hites served in twenty-five of Virginia's sixty-four infantry regiments, in fifteen of Virginia's thirty-one cavalry regiments, and in nine artillery batteries. The Virginia Regimental Histories Series provides details on at least ninety-one Hites from Virginia who fought for the South. Ancestry.com's compilation identifies one hundred two Hites from Virginia who fought for the Confederacy, although no information is available on some beyond their names.[48] However, the two lists do not totally correlate with each other. Details are available on only ninety-one of the one hundred two Hite family members who donned gray—nothing is known of the remaining eleven, who were likely enrolled in local self-defense units. It does not appear that any Hite who grew up in the Shenandoah Valley or elsewhere in Virginia fought for the Union, although four Hites from what would become West Virginia donned the blue uniform and served. Reviewing all available records, well over a hundred Hites from Virginia who fought for the South can be identified, by far the largest contingent from any state.

Hite Participants by Side and State

Confederate

Alabama	15
Arkansas	7
Georgia	11
Kentucky	10
Louisiana	3
Mississippi	2
Missouri	4
North Carolina	5
South Carolina	11
Tennessee	17
Texas	2
Virginia	140
CSA Engineers*	4
TOTAL	231

* State not specified

Union

California	2
Illinois	29
Indiana	37
Iowa	9
Kentucky	12
Maryland	9
Missouri	5
New York	1
Ohio	30
Pennsylvania	51
West Virginia	8
Wisconsin	1
Regular Army	13
USCT	14
Veteran Reserve Corps	13
Union Volunteers	6
TOTAL	240

THE HITE'S CIVIL WAR

Nearly 450 Hites who fought in the Civil War were identified using Ancestry.com's database: 229 Hites who fought to maintain the Union, and 220 who supported the Confederacy, a nearly even split. This, however, is certainly not a comprehensive count, as it is certain that many who fought in the federal ranks are not counted as noted in appendix C, p. 115. Union supporters came from Indiana, Illinois, Ohio, and Pennsylvania, as well as the border states of Maryland, Kentucky, and West Virginia. Two Hites from California enlisted in support of the Union. In addition, thirteen Hites fought in the US Regular Army, and fourteen served with the US Colored Troops.[49] Presumably, the latter were either freed Hite slaves or white officers who led black units. Widespread Hite support for the Union reflects both the continual westward movement of pioneers and the influence of the environment in which one was raised.[50] It should be noted that some soldiers who lived in counties that would become West Virginia fought in regiments and units other than from Virginia—Ohio and Pennsylvania in particular—as well as for the South.

As mentioned, the overwhelming majority of Hites who supported secession came from Virginia (102), but Alabama, Arkansas, Georgia, Kentucky, Louisiana, North and South Carolina, Mississippi, Missouri, Tennessee, and Texas were also represented. The culture where each individual lived had a profound influence on the side supported. Kentucky provided Hites for both sides, as would be expected from a border state.

It is important to note that not all Hites identified in this study are descendants of Jost Hite. Some individuals with the Hite surname were of a different national origin; others stemmed from other branches of the family originating in Germany. A good example of this were the four sons of Conrad Hite (1793–1875) and Margaret Helm (1795–1881) of Puzzletown, Blair County, Pennsylvania. Two of their sons were killed in the course of the war—Private Samuel C. Hite, born December 31, 1835, enlisted in Company A, 55th Pennsylvania Volunteer Infantry Regiment on February 23, 1864. Samuel died of diarrhea on July 16, 1864, in Andersonville Prison in Macon County, Georgia.

HITE PARTICIPATION IN THE CIVIL WAR

Pvt. Samuel C. Hite
55th Pennsylvania Volunteer
Infantry Regiment
Andersonville, Georgia

Samuel's older brother John died on April 2, 1864, during the siege of Petersburg and was buried near the IX Corps field hospital at Meade Station. John was born June 26, 1830, and enlisted August 27, 1864, as a private in Company I, 205th Pennsylvania Volunteer Infantry. Both brothers were married and left families. They also had two other brothers who served but survived the war. Private—later Doctor—David Henry served in Company C, 148th Pennsylvania Volunteer Infantry Regiment from June 1, 1863, to June 24, 1865, and their brother George served in Company A, 89th Pennsylvania Volunteer Infantry Regiment from June 18, 1864, to June 29, 1865.

Their great-grandfather, Johann Heyt, arrived in Philadelphia in 1751 from Grötzingen, Baden-Würtenberg, Germany just east of Karlsruhe, nearly a two-hour train ride from Jost's origin in Bonfeld. The four Hite brothers' grandfather Christopher fought in the Continental Line during the Revolutionary War and was present at the siege at Yorktown, as was Isaac Hite. Thus, this branch of the Hite family originated about fifty miles southwest of Major Hite's forebears' ancestral home. Both came from the state of Baden-Baden, along the northwestern border of the Black Forest mountains. Another Hite family descended from Conrad Heyd and his son Abraham, who emigrated from Kusel in the Rheinland-Phlaz ("The Palatinate") in 1738. No doubt, many other Hites who fought for the North came from these and other

Hite branches whose members had settled north of the Mason-Dixon Line, although clearly some of Jost's descendants who moved westward and no longer lived in a slave-centered environment likely supported the Union cause. In addition, some with a variant of the Hite surname originated from England

Hite family genealogist Richard Hite points out that DNA testing has added a significant new dimension of genealogical research; by 2013 no fewer than 23 separate Heyd/Hoyt family branches had been identified, including 13 who now spell their surname "Hite." In the Shenandoah Valley alone there are eight separate Hite families with absolutely no relationship to Jost Hite's lineage. This study generally ignores all those soldiers who spelled their last names using other common variants (Heydt, Heyd, Heite, Hight, etc.). Given the tendency of the time to spell phonetically, one simply cannot be certain of family affiliation, and of course foreign names were generally anglicized to help with the assimilation process.

Thus, although the data used is a reliable sample, it is not comprehensive because of the nature of surviving documentation and spelling habits. The names given for individuals are not consistent, and there were no serial numbers or name tags to identify soldiers killed in battle. Many soldiers were buried as "unknowns" in common graves. Confederate records in particular provide extremely sketchy details in most cases—the state adjutant general's office was consumed by a fire set by the Confederates as they abandoned Richmond on April 3, 1865, and the military recorder's office, which was responsible for compiling personnel records, was also destroyed the same day. There was no central depository for surviving Confederate documents until the US War Department began to collect and reconstruct them in the 1880s.

As one example (of many) of the inconsistency and unreliable nature of surviving Confederate records, one major study of prominent Virginia families notes that William Meade Hite enlisted at sixteen and was killed in his unit's first engagement a few weeks later.[51] Other sources give his age on enlistment as fourteen and a different date and place of death. The truth is often difficult to reconstruct from the remaining fragments 150 years later.

Surviving records reveal only sketchy biographical outlines for each of Major Hite's grandsons; obtaining details on each is a considerable challenge. Occasionally, entries provide descriptive data on the appearance of an individual. It is striking to note how many Hites are described as "light complexion, blue eyes, light hair," reflecting their Germanic heritage.

"LAST FULL MEASURE"
Four Grandsons, two Great-Grandsons

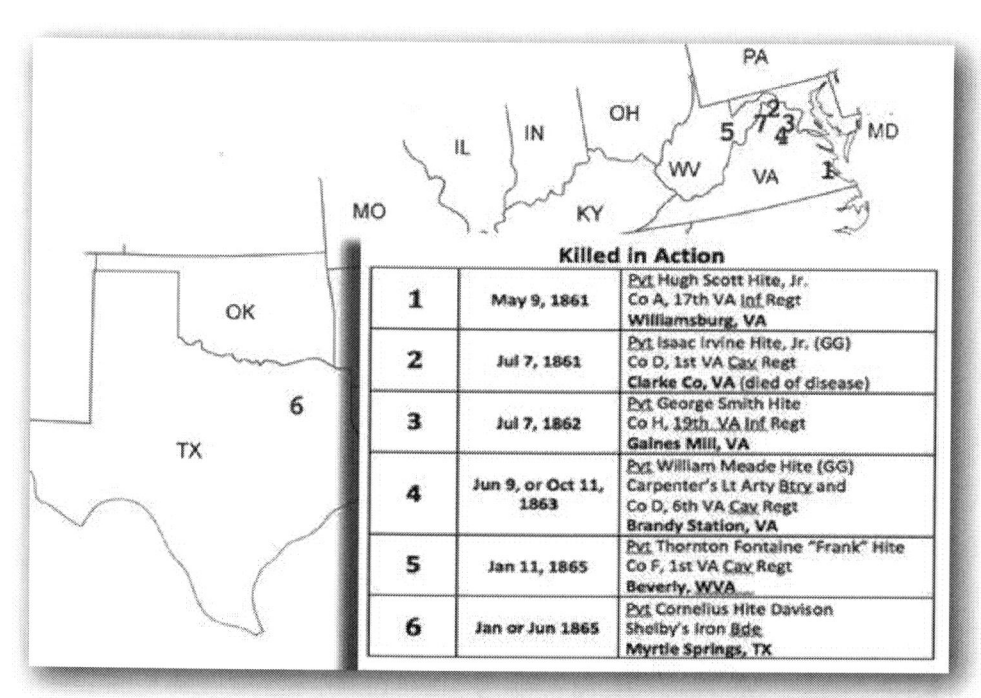

Killed in Action

1	May 9, 1861	Pvt Hugh Scott Hite, Jr. Co A, 17th VA Inf Regt Williamsburg, VA
2	Jul 7, 1861	Pvt Isaac Irvine Hite, Jr. (GG) Co D, 1st VA Cav Regt Clarke Co, VA (died of disease)
3	Jul 7, 1862	Pvt George Smith Hite Co H, 19th VA Inf Regt Gaines Mill, VA
4	Jun 9, or Oct 11, 1863	Pvt William Meade Hite (GG) Carpenter's Lt Arty Btry and Co D, 6th VA Cav Regt Brandy Station, VA
5	Jan 11, 1865	Pvt Thornton Fontaine "Frank" Hite Co F, 1st VA Cav Regt Beverly, WVA
6	Jan or Jun 1865	Pvt Cornelius Hite Davison Shelby's Iron Bde Myrtle Springs, TX

Geographical Disposition of Hite Fatalities

"LAST FULL MEASURE"

1. Cornelius Hite Davison. Cornelius was born on July 8, 1848, at his family's estate, the Forest, in Warren County. If this birth date is correct, he was no more than fourteen years old when he enlisted in General Jo Shelby's Iron Brigade, which fought in the Trans-Mississippi Theater. Cornelius likely died in Myrtle Springs, Texas, about one hundred miles west of present-day Dallas, in May or June 1865, shortly after the war was over. Some genealogists give his date of death as January 10, 1865, but this is unlikely since the unit would probably not have been in Texas at that time. Apparently, he was no more than sixteen years old when he enlisted. No "official" records have been located, and his record of service has been reconstructed from genealogical data and family records alone.

Furthermore, there is a question as to Cornelius's parents. Records indicate that Cornelius was the son of Dr. Alexander McDonald Davison (born at Amber Hill near Winchester in December 1813; died in Jefferson City, Missouri, in March 1889), and Major Hite's youngest daughter, Matilda Madison Hite (born at Belle Grove in June 1819; died in Jefferson City, Missouri, in October 1853). Other records indicate that Cornelius was the son of John Smith "Bull" Davison, a successful lawyer and politician (born in December 1802 at Amber Hill; died in November 1874 at his plantation, the Forest, in Warren County), and Mary Eltinge Hite (born at Belle Grove in October 1808; died at the Forest in February 1866).

John and Alexander Davison were brothers. John Smith "Bull" Davison was the oldest son of John Davison and Sarah Armstrong; his wife, Mary Eltinge Hite, was the second-oldest of Major Hite's ten children by his second wife, Ann Tunstall Maury. Dr. Alexander McDonald Davison and Matilda Madison Hite were the youngest of their families—he was the fourth son of John Davison and Sarah Armstrong's eight children, and Matilda was the last of the six daughters Ann Maury Hite bore with Major Hite.

Dr. Davison and Matilda were most certainly Cornelius's parents. They immigrated to Missouri before the war; Cornelius was about five years old when his mother died. Dr. Davison remarried about two years after her death, and it is quite likely that Cornelius was unable to get along with his stepmother,

Mary Catherine Powell. In any case, he apparently returned east to live with his aunt and uncle, who would have been his parents' older brother and sister. In the 1850 census, Cornelius *E.* Davison is listed last in the family of John Smith "Bull" Davison, out of age order with the other children. However, this individual is listed as being fourteen years old, meaning he would have been born in 1836, a twelve-year difference from the date—1848—genealogists accept for Cornelius's birth. This "Cornelius *E.*" is notably absent in the 1860 census—possibly by then Cornelius had made his way back to Missouri.

As mentioned, Cornelius's service information is more fragmentary than most other Hites. The Virginia Regimental Histories Series has compiled comprehensive data for most individual Virginians who served in Confederate units, but there is nothing like it for Missouri Confederate units, nor for most other Southern states, for that matter.

A passage from one family genealogy *(Cobb Family History, Fifth Generation, Volume III, Chapter V)* observes, "When a bright, attractive boy of sixteen, he became enthusiastic over the attractions of a soldier's life, and joined Shelby's Brigade. In their terrible march to Texas, when strong men succumbed to hunger and fatigue, the boy soldier sank under his privations and died at Myrtle Springs, Texas." Note the age discrepancy—if the birth date given in most genealogies is correct, Cornelius was probably around fourteen, not sixteen years, when he enlisted.[52]

Shelby's Iron Brigade was a Confederate cavalry brigade that fought with distinction in the Trans-Mississippi Theater, a four-hundred-thousand-square mile expanse west of the Mississippi River. Three regiments were brigaded under the command of Colonel (later Major General) Jo Shelby. The Iron Brigade participated in four major raids into Missouri during the war, earning a reputation as the most formidable fighting force in the theater. The brigade moved to Clarksburg, Texas, in November 1864. Rather than surrender with the collapse of the Confederacy in the West in June 1865, General Shelby and most of his brigade rode south to Mexico to offer their services to Emperor Maximilian, who declined their offer. However, Maximilian provided land for an American colony in Mexico, and many of the troopers from Shelby's brigade settled there.[53]

"LAST FULL MEASURE"

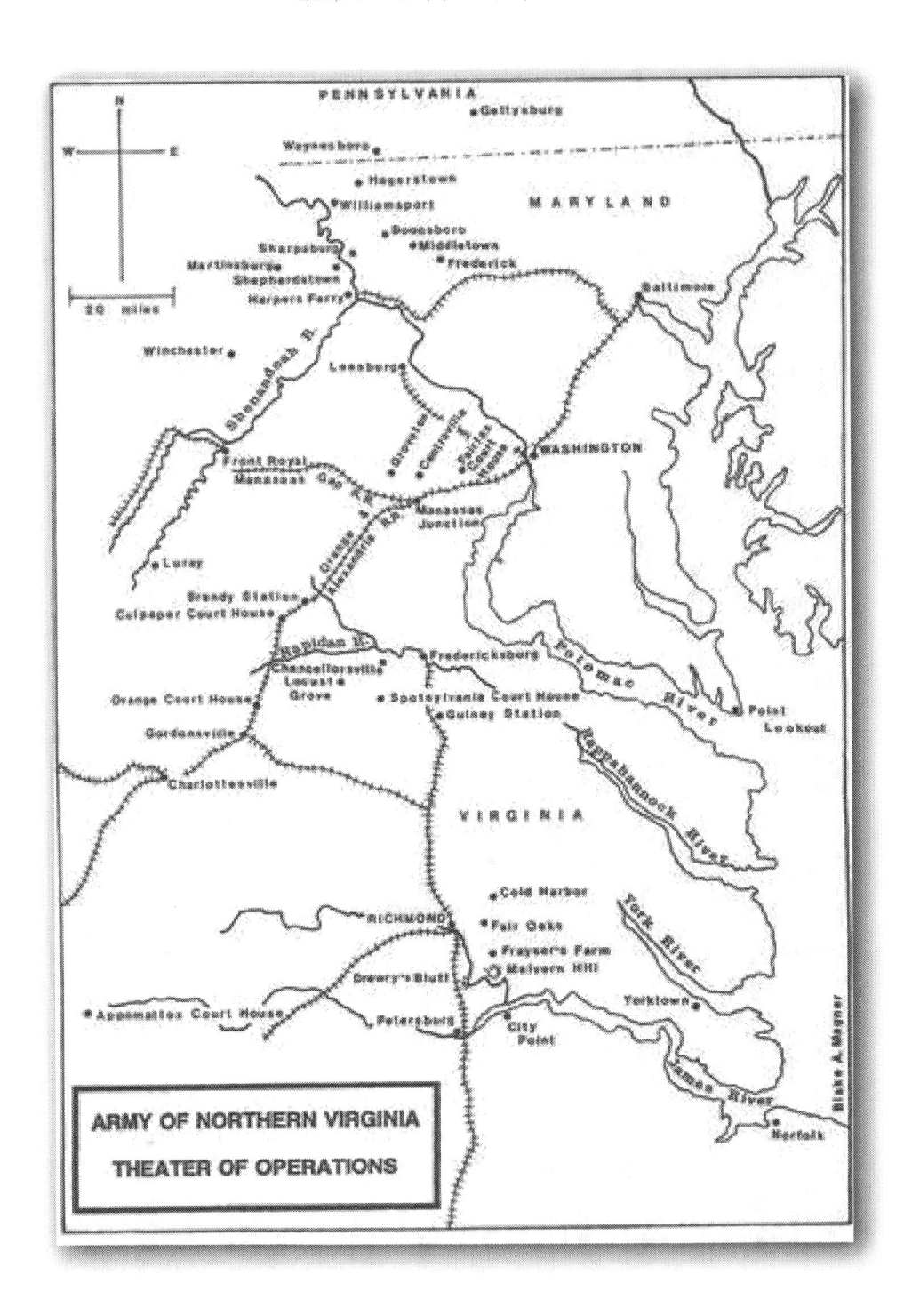

ARMY OF NORTHERN VIRGINIA
THEATER OF OPERATIONS

2. George Smith Hite. George was born on August 19, 1847, in Amherst County. He died July 7, 1862, from wounds suffered at the Battle of Gaines' Mill, one of the Seven Days' Battles of McClellan's Peninsula Campaign. George was the son of Doctor Walker Maury Hite Sr. (born at Belle Grove on May 12, 1811; died April 8, 1890) and Mary Eleanor Williams (born on March 31, 1816; she also died in 1890). Both parents are buried in Grace Episcopal Church Cemetery at Cismont in Albemarle County. George's brothers Isaac Williams, Thornton Fontaine "Frank," and Walker Maury Jr. also fought for the South. Frank likewise gave his life for the Confederacy.

George enlisted as a private at Amherst Court House when he was fourteen years old in Company H, 19th Virginia Infantry Regiment, "The Southern Rights Guards," part of George Pickett's Brigade, on January 28, 1861, well before the outbreak of the Civil War. He was badly wounded with a severely damaged leg in the Battle of Gaines' Mill near Richmond on June 27, 1862, and died on July 7, 1862, while being treated in Chimborazo Hospital in Richmond. He is buried in Hollywood Cemetery in Richmond, where most Confederate burials from Chimborazo Hospital took place.[54] He died a month shy of his fifteenth birthday.

3. Hugh Holmes "Scott" Hite Jr. Hugh was born on March 3, 1839, in Middletown, Frederick County, Virginia, probably at Belle Grove Plantation. Hugh was the son of Hugh Holmes Hite Sr. (born in August 1816, at Belle Grove; died in 1870 in Piedmont in Rappahannock County) and Anne Randolph Meade (born in January 1818, in Clarke County, she died in Virginia sometime after the census of 1860). He was twenty-two years old and a clerk at the time of his enlistment in Prince William County. Apparently, he had lived for a time in Prince William County before moving to Alexandria.

"Scott" enlisted at Alexandria when he was twenty-two years old as a private on April 17, 1861, in Company A, the "Alexandria Riflemen," of the 17th Virginia Infantry Regiment (known as the Bloody Seventeenth). He was wounded and captured after the Battle of Williamsburg on May 5,

1862, and died four days later while in Union hands.[55] His company lost five killed and four wounded in the engagement. He is buried in the Confederate cemetery in Williamsburg. The regiment first fought at Manassas and fell under the command of a succession of commanders—Generals Longstreet, Ewell, A. P. Hill, Kemper, and finally Course—indicative of the cost of the war.

The Terror of War

4. Thornton Fontaine "Frank" Hite was born July 31, 1839, in Middletown, Frederick County, probably at Belle Grove. He was the son of Doctor Walker Maury Hite Sr. (born at Belle Grove in May 1811; died in April 1890 at Kinlock, the family estate in Amherst County) and Mary Eleanor Williams (born in March 1816, in Shenandoah County, she died in 1890). Both are buried in Albemarle County. Fontaine's brothers Isaac Williams and Walker Maury Jr. also fought for the South; his brother George Smith was likewise killed in action.

THE HITE'S CIVIL WAR

On July 2, 1861, "Frank" enlisted as a private in Company F of the 1st Virginia Cavalry Regiment, whose first commander was Colonel J. E. B. Stuart. His cousins Isaac Irvine, Cornelius Baldwin, and James Madison Hite also served in that regiment, most of whom came from Clarke County. Frank was detached as a baggage guard on March 4, 1862, "mustered out" of the regiment on April 18, 1862, and transferred to Company D of the 6th Virginia Cavalry Regiment the same day. At that time, the 1st Cavalry Regiment totaled 437 men. In July 1863 it lost 8 percent of the 310 engaged at Gettysburg, and had 318 fit for duty in September 1864. The 1st Virginia Cavalry cut through the federal lines at Appomattox and disbanded; only one man from the unit surrendered.

Hite was killed in action on January 11, 1865, during a successful Confederate raid on a Union supply depot at Beverly in Randolph County, West Virginia. He was the sole fatality during General Thomas Rosser's raid on the depot, which netted 580 prisoners and a large quantity of badly needed supplies. Hite was shot in the chest and mortally wounded by a federal pistol shot while entering an enemy shelter. He had been advancing dismounted in the hopes of obtaining a horse from federal forces—Southern troopers had to furnish their own mounts.[56]

An unidentified cousin provided an account of this action:

Private Fontaine Hite, of Frederick County, who had enlisted in the Clarke Cavalry, and who had lost his horse, learning that there was a probable opportunity of remounting himself if he accompanied the expedition, did so afoot, walking the entire distance. Going to the door of one of the huts occupied by the sleeping enemy, he kicked it open and walked in. A (Union) soldier, realizing that an attack was being made upon the encampment, seized his pistol and firing at Hite gave him a wound from which he died in a few hours.[57]

In addition to these four grandsons, two of Major Hite's great-grandsons were killed fighting for the South:

"LAST FULL MEASURE"

1. Isaac Irvine Hite Jr. (Records also list him as Isaac E. Hite, another example of the difficulty working with surviving information.) Isaac was born on November 16, 1841, in Clarke County, the son of Isaac Irvine Hite Sr. and Susan Burwell Meade. Isaac Irvine Sr. (Irvine was his mother's maiden name) was born on in February 1820 at Guilford, in Clarke County, the plantation of his father, James Madison Hite Sr., Major Hite and Nelly Madison's surviving son. Isaac Irvine Sr. apparently died in Florida; his date of death is unknown. Susan Meade was born around 1821 and died when she was only thirty years old, in February 1852, leaving her husband six children to raise. Isaac was about eleven years old when his mother died. His brother, William Meade Hite, also died fighting for the Confederacy.

Isaac enlisted as a private in Company D, 1st Virginia Cavalry Regiment on May 15, 1861, serving under J. E. B. Stuart, the regiment's first colonel. Irvine died of disease on July 1, 1861, in Clarke County, little more than a month after he enlisted. Records reflect only that he was "mustered out" on July 1, 1861, in Clarke County.[58]

As soon as the roughly five thousand troops of General Joseph Johnston's army began concentrating around Winchester in April 1861, measles, mumps, smallpox, scarlet fever, and typhoid fever broke out among the soldiers. At least two soldiers, one a Private John Hite, complained that the local drinking water "maid (*sic*) the boys very sick."[59] Fully one-third of the 33rd Virginia Infantry Regiment came down with measles.[60] Isaac's death only a month and a half after he enlisted reflects the high mortality rate of troops because of disease through the war. There were actually more deaths because of illness rather than combat throughout the war. Isaac is buried in the family plot at Meade Memorial Episcopal Church Cemetery at White Post in Clarke County.[61]

The effects of disease and constant attrition from field service can be seen in the fact that by April 1862, the regiment consisted of 437 men out of a normal 1,000-man complement. The 1st Virginia Cavalry lost 8 percent of the 318 men engaged at Gettysburg in July 1863 and had 318 men fit for duty in September 1864. Neither army had regular replacement systems during the war. As previously mentioned, only one man from the regiment surrendered at Appomattox.[62]

2. William Meade Hite was born November 9, 1847 in Clarke County and most likely killed or wounded on June 9, 1863, at Brandy Station. William was the son of Isaac Irvine Hite Sr. (born in February 1820, died in Orange County, Florida, unknown) and Susan Burwell Meade (born May 1, 1821, in Clarke County, she died in February 185.) She was only thirty years old and left Isaac Sr. six children to raise; William was about eight when his mother died. Isaac Sr.'s father was James Madison Hite, Nelly Madison's son. Thus, not only was William Major Hite's great-grandson, but he was President James Madison's "great-grand nephew" as well. William's brother, Isaac Irvine Hite Jr. (see above), likewise lost his life fighting for the Southern cause.

William enlisted as a private on April 20, 1861, in Captain Carpenter's Light Artillery Battery, the "Alleghany Roughs," when he was fourteen years old. He originally served in the 27th Infantry Regiment, but was soon selected to serve in the artillery. Private Hite was most likely killed at Brandy Station on June 9, 1863, but may not have been serving in the battery at the time. One document, a postwar register of the 6th Virginia Cavalry Regiment, lists a William M. Hite from Frederick County who served in the regiment's Company D, said to have been killed on October 11, 1863, "in the battle at Brandy Station."[63] The battle at Brandy Station, the largest cavalry engagement of the war, took place on June 9 and was the opening engagement of General Robert E. Lee's campaign into Pennsylvania, which culminated at Gettysburg the first three days of July 1863. There is also a good possibility that William subsequently died of wounds sustained during the battle.

Cavalry Melee at Brandy Station

The 6th Cavalry regimental roster lists William M. Hite's place of enlistment as Albemarle County, causing some uncertainty that this is the same William Meade Hite, since the 1860 census placed him in Clarke County. However, other documents give his residence as Albemarle County. Unfortunately, not all the pieces of historical puzzles fit precisely.

THE SURVIVORS

NINE GRANDSONS, A GREAT-GRANDSON, AND FIFTY-THREE OTHER VIRGINIA HITES

1. Dr. Robert Stuart Baldwin He was born in 1824 at Cedar Grove, today's Heater House, next to Belle Grove, the son of Dr. Cornelius Elijah Baldwin Jr. (December 1790–September 1828) and Eleanor "Nelly" Conway Hite (December 1789–August 1830). Nelly was the only daughter of Isaac's first wife, President James Madison's sister, after whom she was named.

Dr. Robert Stuart Baldwin Sr.

Dr. Baldwin was born April 15, 1824, completed his medical studies at the University of Virginia, marrying Letitia Jane Speck in 1847. They had six children, all but one born before the war. He enlisted in the Confederate army on March 13, 1862, when he was thirty-seven years old, leaving behind a wife and four children. He served as assistant surgeon at Pratt Hospital in Lynchburg and in other Virginia locations until he was assigned as surgeon to the 16th North Carolina Infantry Regiment, part of General A. P. Hill's corps. On December 7, 1863, he tendered his resignation as surgeon in the Provisional Army of the Confederate States, "partly from the frequent solicitations from the community who are almost entirely destitute of medical aid, but more particularly from private considerations of the most cogent necessity."[64] The resignation was accepted twelve days later. Interestingly, he was promoted to full surgeon in March 1865. The cause for Baldwin's resignation was probably the sickness of his son, Cornelius Hite Baldwin, who died at sixteen in 1864.

Limited information suggests that wartime trauma may have left its mark. Robert practiced medicine in a number of locations after the war until he entered the Robert E. Lee Camp Confederate Veterans' Soldiers Home in August 1889. He died nine years later on July 14, 1898, at the home of one of his daughters in Gretna, Pittsylvania County, located on the North Carolina border, in July 1898. Dr. Baldwin is buried in an unmarked grave; his wife died an inmate in a church home in Richmond in 1907.

2. Isaac Hite Bird Isaac was born in Woodstock, Shenandoah County, in 1845, the son of Mark Bird Sr. (December 1810–January 1883) and Sarah Clark Macon Hite (November 1812–July 1896). His brother, Sergeant Mark Bird Jr. (below), fought in the 10th Virginia Infantry Regiment.

Isaac enlisted as a private in Company C, 7th Virginia Cavalry Regiment, commanded by Colonel Turner Ashby, and was captured early in the war. When he was released, he joined Company D, 23rd Cavalry Regiment on September 23,1863. He was captured once more at Woodstock on January 11, 1865, and was imprisoned at Fort McHenry, Baltimore, spending the rest of the war as a POW until he took the oath of allegiance on May 1, 1865.

Private Isaac Hite Bird

After the war, he became a prominent attorney in Shenandoah County. He married Leila Zirkle on November 24, 1881. They had four children, two of whom died within a year of birth; the other two died at nine and twenty-five years of age. He died of heart complications December 7, 1892. Reporting on his funeral, Harrisonburg's *Rockingham Register* noted that he had filled "numerous positions of public trust." He is buried in Massanutten Cemetery.[65]

3. Sergeant Mark Bird Jr. He was born on May 25, 1836, in Woodstock, Shenandoah County, the son of Judge Mark Bird (December 1810–January 1883) and Sarah Clark Macon Hite (November 1812–July 1896). Mark's brother Isaac Hite Bird, above, originally fought in Ashby's 7th Virginia Cavalry Regiment.

Mark attended at least two years of university prior to the outbreak of war. He enlisted as "2nd corporal" in Company F, 10th Virginia Infantry Regiment on April 18, 1861, and was subsequently promoted to "3rd sergeant" in May 1863. He was wounded at Gettysburg in July 1863, returning to his unit around February 1864. He was wounded a second time at the Wilderness on May 5, 1864. He transferred to Company B at the end of October and was captured during the last Confederate attack around Petersburg, at Fort Steadman on March 25, 1865. He was imprisoned at Point Lookout, Maryland, and released upon taking the oath of allegiance on June 23.

THE SURVIVORS

Mark was five feet six and three-quarter inches tall, had a fair complexion, dark-brown hair, and gray eyes. He farmed after the war and died unmarried in Woodstock on February 25, 1903. Given his education and selection for leadership in his regiment, it seems remarkable that he chose to farm and did not marry after the war. This may be a reflection of the heavy toll exacted by being twice wounded and imprisoned. He too is buried in Massanutten Cemetery.[66]

4. Cornelius Baldwin "Nealy" Hite Jr. Cornelius was born on August 5, 1842, at Belle Grove Plantation in Frederick County. He was the son of Cornelius Baldwin Hite Sr. (born in February 1818, died at 23 years of age in a hunting accident in November 1841) and Elizabeth Augusta Smith (born in November 1818, died in 1900).

Cornelius enlisted as a private from Clarke County on July 2, 1861, in Company F, 1st Virginia Cavalry Regiment. His cousin Thornton Fontaine "Frank" Hite enlisted in the same regiment the same day. For some reason, Cornelius was "mustered out"—apparently discharged—on December 17, 1861. Nealy served as acting lieutenant of topographical engineers under C. S. Dwight in Lynchburg during 1863, resigning sometime later that year. He reenlisted on March 26, 1864, and was assigned to Company D, 6th Virginia Cavalry Regiment. He was sick and confined to the hospital on September 10, 1864, and was listed as absent without leave on the roll call for March 25, 1865.

42

Interestingly, Nealy's picture is in both 1st and 6th Cavalry regimental histories—but identified as a different person in each volume! The trooper wearing a kepi on the right in the 6th Cavalry Regiment's history is identified as "Cornelius B. Hite of Company D." However, the regimental history of the 1st Cavalry Regiment identifies that individual as Archibald Magill Smith—Cornelius's uncle, who was seven years Cornelius's senior. There is no way of being certain which is correct.

After the war, Cornelius farmed in Fauquier County until 1880 and then worked in the Pension Bureau. He was reportedly a teacher, surveyor, realtor, and engaged in selling mortgages and insurance. He lived in Washington, DC, for a number of years and was active in Confederate veterans' activities. He died at age 101 in the Soldiers Home in Richmond on October 9, 1943, and is buried in Hollywood Cemetery in Richmond.[67]

5. Cornelius Randolph Hite Sr. was born April 7, 1845. Cornelius was a farmer from Rappahannock County and the son of Hugh Holmes Hite Sr. (1816–1870) and Anne Randolph Meade (January 11, 1811–about 1860). Thomas Jefferson's mother was a Randolph. Cornelius died on November 2, 1918, in Rappahannock County and is buried in the Saint Paul Episcopal Church Cemetery in Woodville.

Cornelius enlisted as a private on March 20, 1863, in H Company, 4th Virginia Cavalry Regiment, when he was about seventeen years old. His horse was killed at Stevensburg on October 11, 1863, and he was captured in Fauquier County on February 6, 1864. He was imprisoned first at the Old Capitol Prison in Washington, DC, and then transported to Elmira Prison in upstate New York on August 12, 1864. He was released at Gainesville on June 19, 1865, and married Elizabeth "Lizzie" Catherine Stark on November 3, 1874. He died on November 2, 1918, in Rappahannock County and is buried in the Saint Paul Episcopal Church Cemetery in Woodville.[68] His widow applied for a pension in May 1924 when she was eighty-two years old. Cornelius stood five feet nine, had hazel eyes, dark hair, and a fair complexion.

6. Isaac Williams Hite Born October 28, 1837, Isaac was a farmer from Amherst County. He was the son of Doctor Walker Maury Hite Sr. (born May 1811, died in April 1890 at his estate, Kinlock, in Amherst County) and Mary Eleanor Williams (born March 1816, she died sometime in 1890). His brothers Walker Maury Jr., Fontaine Thornton "Frank," and George Smith also fought for the South; the latter two were killed in action.

Isaac was twenty-four years old when he enlisted as a private in Company H, 19th Virginia Infantry Regiment at Amherst Court House on April 15, 1861. He was promoted to "2nd corporal" on August 15, 1863, and promoted to full corporal on October 15, 1863. He was transferred to the 62nd Virginia Infantry Regiment on July 21, 1864. Records state simply that he was "mustered out," providing no further information.[69] Isaac was drawing a pension in 1920 and died sometime after 1930.

7. James Madison Hite Jr. James was the son of James Madison Hite Sr. (May 11, 1825–January 11, 1860), Major Isaac Hite's third child, and the only surviving son with James Madison's sister Nelly. His mother was Caroline Matilda Irvine (born September 5, 1789, in Lynchburg; died March 11, 1877 in Staunton). James was a gentleman farmer from the Berryville/Millwood area of Clarke County and the grandnephew of President James Madison as well as Major Hite's grandson. James was born at his father's estate, Guilford Plantation, on May 11, 1825.

"Madison" enlisted in Company D, 1st Virginia Cavalry Regiment, on April 18, 1861, but was "mustered out" on May 15, 1861, and discharged on July 8, 1861, because he hired a substitute named Sigismund Zulasky to serve in his place. This was a common practice for plantation owners owning slaves. Anyone with more than twenty slaves was exempted from military service, a reflection of Southern concern for slave rebellion and the need to maintain plantations' productivity to support the war effort. The policy did not help the morale of small-scale farmers drafted into the Confederate army who enjoyed no such exemption.

James received mail from a Front Royal post office after the war, and the 1870 census listed his residence as Warren County. He became a successful realtor and died in Baltimore on March 10, 1892.[70]

8. Kidder Meade Hite Kidder was born May 11, 1840, and was a clerk from Alexandria when he enlisted at twenty years of age. Kidder was the son of Hugh Holmes Hite Sr. (born in August 1816, died in Rappahannock County in 1870) and Anne Randolph Meade (born in January 1818, Anne died in Prince William County sometime after the census of 1860).

Kidder enlisted when he was twenty, on April 17, 1861, in Company M, 17th Virginia Infantry Regiment (the "Bloody Seventeenth"), the same regiment in which his cousin Hugh Holmes Hite served. He was promoted to corporal on December 1, 1863, captured at Petersburg on April 2, 1865, and sent to Point Lookout, Maryland. He was released on June 13, 1865, after taking the loyalty oath and died on January 23, 1896, in Culpeper County.[71]

9. Walker Maury Hite Jr. He was born about 1848 in Amherst County, the son of Doctor Walker Maury Hite Sr. (born in May 1811, died in Amherst County in April 1890) and Mary Eleanor Williams (born in March 1816 and died in Amherst County in 1890). Three of his brothers, Isaac Williams, Fontaine Thornton "Frank," and George Smith Hite, also served; the latter two were killed fighting for the South.

Walker enlisted as a private in 1863 in Lamkin's Battery of the Amherst-Nelson Light Artillery. Not much is available regarding his military service; the battery's history merely notes "appears on a roster of POWs surrendered and paroled on April 9, 1865, at Appomattox Court House."[71]

At least one great grandson, **William Smith Davison,** fought for the South and survived the war, losing an arm at Fishers Hill (September 22, 1864.). Davison was born in Jefferson City, Missouri, on October 4, 1845, and died in Walla Walla, Washington, on November 29, 1904. William was the son of Edward Jaquelin Davison (born in May 1805; died in September 1848) and Eleanor Conway Baldwin (born in March 1810; died in August 1849), the granddaughter of Major Hite and his first wife, Eleanor "Nellie" Conway Madison. William was thus also President Madison's grandnephew.

William's parents moved to Jefferson City, Missouri, decades before the war. William's father died when he was three, and his mother died the following year, both of unknown causes, leaving their three children orphans. William and his sister, Eleanor Cornelia Davison, were adopted by Dr. Cornelius Elijah Baldwin Jr. and Eleanor "Nelly" Conway Hite, who lived in Frederick County. Their younger sister, Edmonia Louise Davison, was adopted by their aunt Ann Maury Baldwin, wife of the US consul in Jaffa, Syria. They were joined by Ann's sister, Mary Briscoe Baldwin, a missionary for the Episcopal Church in Syria. Edmonia died near Athens, Greece, when she was eight years old.

Losing both parents while he was still a toddler must have been a heavy blow. His sister Eleanor felt she was mistreated by her foster parents and married a man thirteen years older than she to escape her situation. According to family lore, William left home when he was fourteen years old to join the Confederate army. However, comparing his birth date and enlistment suggests that he was actually closer to eighteen.

William enlisted in Company D of the 23rd Virginia Cavalry Regiment on November 7, 1863, part of the Northwestern (Partisan) Brigade commanded by General John D. Imboden of Major General Lunsford L. Lomax's Cavalry Division. The 23rd Virginia Cavalry was authorized under the Partisan Ranger Act of April 28, 1862. These irregulars were essentially privateers—they were entitled to receive a share of the goods they captured. They rarely drilled and did not have the discipline of regular cavalry units. The nature of the unit also mitigated against accurate record keeping.[73] General Robert E. Lee regarded these irregulars as "more an injury than a benefit to the service." General Jubal Early, commander of the Army of the Valley, dismissed these relatively undisciplined units as "Buttermilk Rangers," blaming much of his misfortune in battle in September (Third Battle of Winchester and Fishers Hill) and October 1864 (Toms Brook and Cedar Creek) on the poor performance of his cavalry. The cavalry divisions of Generals Rosser and Lomax were badly whipped on October 9, 1864, in the cavalry action at Toms Brook, sometimes called "The Woodstock Races."

William Smith Davison

Available records contain two discrepancies: William is listed in the regimental history as "William *D*. Davi*d*son." It is likely that both letters are simple clerical errors. Davison is listed as present on muster rolls from August 1 to October 31, 1864. The record for William *D*. Davi*d*son notes "listed as arm off—wounded at Fishers Hill." Davison's tombstone notes that he lost an arm at Fishers Hill fighting under Jubal Early on September 22, 1864.[74] Further evidence is provided by a descendant's note indicating that among "Aunt Edmonia's keepsakes" was a flattened bullet believed to be the one that shattered her father's right arm "near Belle Grove, Middletown, Virginia." There is also a locket with a picture, presumably of

William Smith Davison as a young man, apparently the same person as the photo on the previous page.

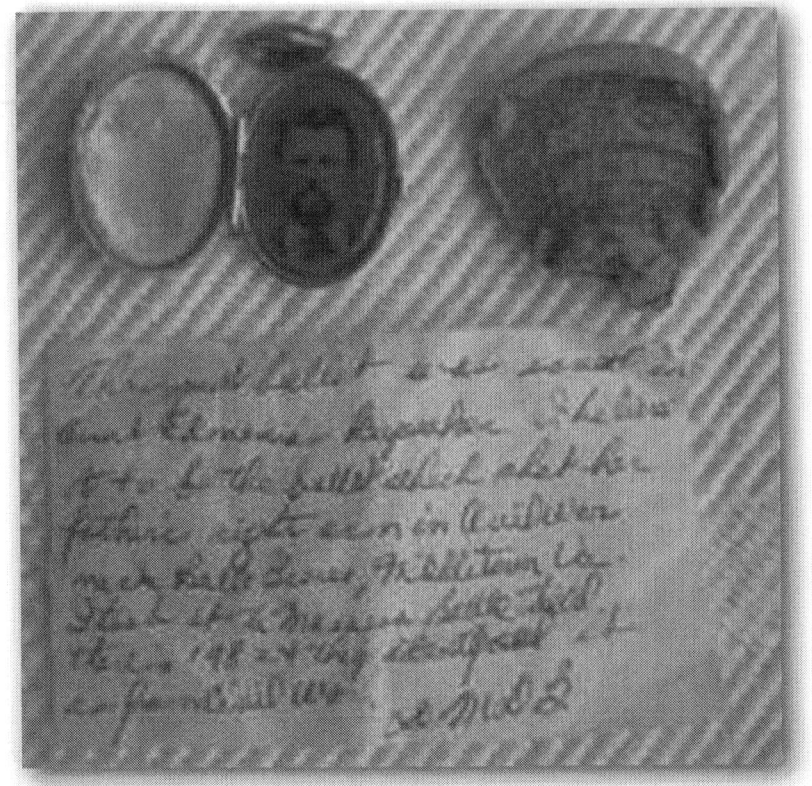

Note written by the niece of William Smith Davison's oldest daughter, Edmonia

Records note that Davison was not present for duty after the last day of October 1864, probably reflecting the fact that, after some time in a hospital for convalescence, he returned home as the war came to an end. General Sheridan captured the remaining fragments of the Army of the Valley, including General Thomas Rosser's cavalry command, at Waynesboro on March 2, 1865. After the Confederate disaster at Fishers Hill, historians note that "many Confederates went home and simply gave up." After the string of Confederate defeats by Sheridan's Army of the Shenandoah in the fall of 1864, Mark Snell quotes Private Grenville Mann from the 30th Virginia Infantry Regiment: "I got out of that Stampede (*sic*) at Fishers Hill on the 22nd of September. Some of our men went to the mountain and just got in today...I was the only one in my company." Mann continued, "Our division is as small now as our brigade was last spring." He noted that morale in the ranks was at a new low.[75]

Davison returned to Missouri in 1867, resuming his education. He taught school and worked in various clerical positions until 1874, when he began reading law and was admitted to the bar. During this time he filled the position of city registrar. Having passed the bar, he began a successful law practice and became successively associate justice of the county court, city attorney, and county prosecuting attorney. Later, he joined Hites from various branches of the family and relocated to Washington State, just as his parents moved to Missouri a generation earlier. His postwar prominence provides evidence of the power of education, as well as the consequences of its absence.

Inscription: "23rd Virginia, Lomax Division under Gen Early, lost his arm at the Battle of Fishers Hill"

WAR'S AFTERMATH

Once the war was over, former Confederates struggled to resume their lives, and the Hite family was no exception. The war produced many invalids as a result of four years of ferocious combat—according to official records, at least 280,000 Union veterans returned home with wounds of varying severity, including some fifty thousand amputees. Estimates place Confederate wounded at somewhat more than half that number. There are no estimates of those who came home with deep psychological wounds or so debilitated by their war experience that they were unable to hold a job. The war engendered a certain amount of postwar lawlessness. Two Hite brothers, Clarence and Robert Woodson "Wood" Hite, rode with Jesse and Frank James, their cousins. Jesse and "Wood" had served in Quantrell's notorious Confederate partisan group during the war, and in the war's aftermath recruited a band who robbed stagecoaches, banks, and trains throughout the West. The two cousins, Jesse and "Wood," were shot dead by a fellow outlaw, while their brothers served jail time.

THE HITE'S CIVIL WAR

Wood Hite
from cover of "Life and Trial of Frank James"

"...a great admirer of himself, as well as of the opposite sex..." --from Triplett

"When did they first commence coming there?" "About 1865, and some of them have been here nearly every year since." - quote of George T. Hite (brother of Clarence & Wood Hite) about the James brothers visits to the Hite home in Adairville, Kentucky --from Triplett

WANTED DEAD OR ALIVE
$5,000.00 FOR THE CAPTURE OF THE MEN WHO ROBBED THE BANK AT NORTHFIELD MINN.
BELIEVED TO BE JESSE JAMES AND HIS BAND OR THE YOUNGERS. THESE MEN ARE DESPERATE.

JESSE OR FRANK JAMES
NOTORIOUS ROBBER OF TRAINS AND BANKS
$5,000.00 REWARD

    In keeping with their position and heritage, the Hites of Virginia had fully embraced the Southern cause, suffering the same devastating consequences the South endured, a high death rate, displacement, and tremendous economic disruption in the postwar years. While the true human or economic cost of the war will never be known precisely (military casualties continue to be adjusted upward), the Civil War Trust estimates that up to 490,300 Southerners lost their lives, were wounded, imprisoned, or missing out of some 592,000 who served. For every three soldiers killed in battle, five more died of sickness. The Trust estimates that fewer than six thousand Southern men of military age escaped military service. Union casualties were 596,000 out of 1,532,000 who served. Overall, 2 percent of the US population died in battle of wounds or sickness, equal to about six million soldiers in today's population. Even if one survived a wound, any projectile that hit bone in either an arm or a leg almost invariably necessitated amputation. Available data indicates that there were also over fifty thousand civilian casualties.

WAR'S AFTERMATH

In four years, there had been some 10,455 military engagements, some catastrophic in human life, plus naval clashes, accidents, suicides, sicknesses, murders, and executions resulting in 1,094,453 casualties. As historian James M. McPherson notes, deaths directly associated with the Civil War were greater than all of America's wars combined up to Vietnam.

In January 1863, the U.S. government estimated that the war was costing $2.5 million daily. In 1865, the national debt stood at $2.7 billion. The annual interest on that debt alone was more than twice our entire national budget in 1860 and was almost twice what the federal government spent before 1860. A final official estimate in 1879 of Union war costs totaled $6,190 billion; the Confederacy spent perhaps $2,100 billion. By 1906, an additional $3.3 billion had been spent by the U.S. government on pensions and other veterans' benefits for former Federal soldiers. Southern states and private philanthropy provided benefits to the Confederate veterans. The amount spent on benefits eventually exceeded the war's original cost.

Inflation affected both North and South, but hit the Confederacy much harder. Northern currency fluctuated in value, and at its lowest point $2.59 in Federal paper money equaled one dollar in gold. The Confederate currency so declined in purchasing power that eventually $60-$70 equaled a gold dollar, making Confederate currency essentially worthless.

Almost all of the South was devastated: burned or plundered homes, pillaged countryside, incalculable losses in crops and farm animals, ruined buildings, bridges, railroads, devastated college campuses, and neglected roads all left the South in ruins. Detailed studies of Union and Confederate military casualties are found in *Numbers and Losses in the Civil War in America 1861-65* by Thomas L. Livermore (1901) and *Regimental Losses in the American Civil War, 1867-1865* by William F. Fox (1889).

Four years of combat in the Valley left most Valley farms devastated. Fence rails, outbuildings, and forests had been used for camp fires, corduroy roads, or winter shelters by both armies. Sheridan's successful campaign of the fall of 1864 resulted in "The Burning"—destruction of more than seventy grist mills and two thousand barns filled with that year's harvest. Union troops also seized or slaughtered thousands of cattle, sheep, hogs, and poultry for a distance of some 140 miles, from Rockbridge County to the Potomac River. Sherman's campaign in the Valley preceded Sherman's "hard war" across Georgia, which began shortly afterward.

The loss of six out of the sixteen family members directly descended from Isaac who served in the Confederate army, a loss of about 37 percent, was somewhat greater than McPherson's calculation that a quarter of all serving Confederate soldiers died during the war. It is important to remember that these calculations are based on estimates, so casual was record keeping, particularly for illness.

Little is known of the effect the war had on Hite farm holdings, but it can be assumed that the family suffered the same fate as most. In general, very few Southern families lived lives of genteel prosperity in the postwar years. When the Commonwealth of Virginia enacted a series of pension acts between 1888 and 1934, it made a great difference to the lives some Hites, even though these pensions did not provide large sums, typically several dollars per month.

ENDNOTES

1. Bryant R. Harper, *A Factual History of Education in Winchester, Virginia* (Charlottesville: University of Virginia, unpublished thesis, October 1944), 78.

2. Rebecca A. Ebert and Teresa Lazazzera, *Frederick County, Virginia: From the Frontier to the Future: A Pictorial History* (Norfolk, Virginia: The Donning Company, 1988), 158.

3. Charles S. Sydnor, *A History of the South: Development of Southern Sectionalism, 1819–1848*, Vol. VIII (Baton Rouge: Louisiana State University Press, 1948), 57–59.

4. Ibid.

5. Ibid., 59.

6. Ibid.

7. Sadie Bell, *The Church, the State, and Education in Virginia* (Science Press Printing Company, 1930), 334.

8. J. E. Norris, editor, *History of the Lower Shenandoah Valley* (Berryville, Virginia: A. Warner and Company, 1890), 213.

9. Sydnor, *A History of the Deep South*, 59.

10. James M. McPherson, *Ordeal by Fire: Volume III, Reconstruction* (New York: Alfred A. Knopf, 1982), 611.

11. Ibid., 612.

ENDNOTES

12. Ronald L. Heinemann, John G. Kolp, Anthony S. Parent Jr., and William G. Shade, *Old Dominion, New Commonwealth: A History of Virginia, 1607–2007* (Charlottesville: University of Virginia Press, 2007), 279 and 301.

13. McPherson, *Ordeal by Fire*, 611.

14. Henry Irving Tragle, *The Southampton Slave Revolt of 1831: A Compilation of Source Material, Including the Full Text of the Confessions of Nat Turner* (Amherst, Massachusetts: The University of Massachusetts Press, 1971), 479.

15. Richard R. Duncan, *Beleaguered Winchester: A Virginia Community at War, 1861–1865* (Baton Rouge: Louisiana State University Press, 2007), 4.

16. Ibid., 3.

17. Sydnor, *A History of the Deep South*, 59.

18. Sydnor, *A History of the South*, 59, and Margaretta Barton Colt, *Defend the Valley: A Shenandoah Family in the Civil War. Defend the Valley* (New York: Orion Books, 1994), 71. Ironically, the writer of the letter, David Walker Barton, a successful lawyer and farmer, was the current owner of Springdale, the home built by Colonel John Hite in 1753. The Barton family purchased it around 1800. The building in enrolled in the National Register of Historic Places

19. Hal F. Sharpe, *Shenandoah County in the Civil War: Four Dark Years* (Charleston, South Carolina: The History Press, 2012), 41.

20. George L. Sherwood and Jeffrey C. Weaver, *20th, 39th, and Virginia Infantry Regiments* (Lynchburg, Virginia: H. E. Howard Publishing Company Inc. 1994), 3.

21. Ibid.

22. Wikipedia, http://en.wikipedia.org/wiki/Wide_Awakes.

23. Thomas A. Ashby, *The Valley Campaign, Being the Reminiscences of a Non-Combatant between the Lines in the Shenandoah Valley during the War of the States* (Neale Publishing House, 1914), 12, 134.

24. Ibid., 19.

25. Jennie Bourne, Carleton University. "Slavery in the United States," EH.net, Economic History Association (http://eh.net/encyclopedia/article/wahl.slavery.us).

26. Ibid.

27. Jonathan A Noyalas, *Two Peoples, One Community: The African American Experience in Newtown (Stephens City), Virginia, 1850–1860* (Stephens City, Virginia: The Stone House Foundation, 2007), 7.

28. Warren R. Hofstra, *A Separate Place: The Formation of Clarke County, Virginia* (Madison, Wisconsin: Madison House Publishers, 1999), 27, Annex B, 111.

29. Ibid., 14.

30. Sharpe, *Shenandoah County*, 28.

31. Ibid., 32.

32. Ibid., 30.

33. Ibid., 69.

34. National Daily Intelligencer, Washington, DC, 09-8-1824, Vol. XII, Issue 3632, 1.

ENDNOTES

35. 1850 Census Slave Schedule, Frederick County.

36. Warren R. Hofstra, *The Planting of New Virginia: Settlement and Landscape in the Shenandoah Valley.* (Baltimore: The Johns Hopkins Press, 2004), 335.

37. Ibid., 336.

38. Ibid., 337.

39. Hofstra, *A Separate Place*, 101–112.

40. This was due in large part to the policy of Robert Carter, agent for Lord Fairfax, who granted large areas in eastern Frederick County to Tidewater planters, including himself and his kin. See Hofstra, *A Separate Place*, and Mitchell, *Appalachian Families*.

41. Hofstra, *A Separate Place*, 111.

42. Ibid., 69.

43. Ibid., 95.

44. Heinemann, *Old Dominion, New Commonwealth*, 203. Whereas in 1840, 80 percent of Virginians worked on farms, by the 1850 census, only 48 percent of Virginia's free male population were farmers or planters, while just over 20 percent of that entire cohort were listed as laborers. Many farms in Virginia, in the Shenandoah Valley in particular, were worked by "planters" and small farmers, including some Hites. An important factor impacting both the decline of the slave population and the number of farmers was Cyrus McCormick's invention of the mechanical reaper in Rockbridge County in 1831, along with the steady invention of other labor-saving devices.

45. Jerry W. Holsworth, *Civil War Winchester* (Charleston, South Carolina: The History Press, 2011), 20.

46. Ibid.

47. Margaretta Barton Colt. *Defend the Valley: A Shenandoah Family in the Civil War.* (New York: Orion Books, 1994), 409.

48. Janet B. Hewett, *The Roster of Confederate Soldiers, 1861–1865*, Vol. VIII, Wilmington, North Carolina: Broadfoot Publishing Company, 1995, 41 and 42; Ancestry.com.

49. US Colored Troops were a critical factor in the outcome of the war, and by 1865 constituted roughly two hundred thousand men, fully 10 percent of the Union's strength, organized into 138 infantry, 6 cavalry, and 14 artillery regiments. In addition to the USCT, black volunteer units were raised in several states (notably, the storied 54th Massachusetts Volunteer Infantry Regiment of "Glory" fame) for a total of 175 black regiments. Freed slaves proved themselves to be good soldiers and made a significant difference in the Union war effort. USCT were initially employed in convoy and guard duty, but later proved to be extremely capable soldiers in their own right. After the Civil War, black troops were legendary as "Buffalo Soldiers" in the Indian wars in the West.

In addition to denying the South economic potential by reducing the workforce on plantations, farms, factories, and industrial enterprises, runaway slaves deprived the Southern armed forces of military support (teamsters, engineers, etc.). Late in the war, the South tried to raise black troops, but this effort encountered much resistance because it was seen as fundamentally antithetical to the South's reliance on the peculiar institution. In any case, the South's effort to organize black troops was a matter of "too little, too late."

ENDNOTES

50. Data available on Hite family participants in the Civil War available through Ancestry.com demonstrates the remarkable dispersal as well as the exponential growth of the Hite family by the time of the fifth generation in North America. Clearly, each individual's allegiance was determined in large part by the culture and environment in which one grew up.

51. Louise Pecquet du Bellet, Some Prominent Virginia Families, Vol. IV (Lynchburg, Virginia: J. P. Bell Company, 1907). (Google Internet Archive).

52. *Cobb Family History, fifth generation, Vol. VIII, Chapter V.* (Ancestry.com).

53. Arthur Anthony, *General Jo Shelby's March* (New York: Random House, 2012); Wikipedia; and Ancestry.com.

54. Ervin L. Jordan Jr., and Herbert A. Thomas Jr., *19th Virginia Infantry Regiment* (Lynchburg, Virginia: H. E. Howard Publishing Company Inc., 1990), 76.

55. Lee A. Wallace Jr., *17th Virginia Infantry Regiment* (Lynchburg, Virginia: H. E. Howard Publishing Company Inc., 1990), 79, 85. Regiments generally started the war with a full complement of around 1,100 men. When the 17th fought at Manassas, it had an initial present-for-duty strength of 745 all ranks, excluding sick, soldiers on details, or under arrest. When the regiment surrendered at Appomattox Court House on April 9,1865, the entire brigade, of which the regiment was a part, totaled 294 officers and enlisted men. By war's end, nine men remained from A Company, and there were no survivors from E Company, according to the regimental history.

56. Robert J. Driver Jr., *1st Virginia Cavalry Regiment* (Lynchburg, Virginia: H. E. Howard Publishing Company Inc., 1991), 186. The 1st Cavalry Regiment was organized at Winchester, Virginia, in July 1861. Unlike

most regiments, the regiment contained twelve companies, drawn from Frederick, Berkeley, Rockbridge, Clarke, Washington, Augusta, Jefferson, Amelia, Loudoun, Rockingham, and Gloucester counties. After taking part in First Manassas, the unit was brigaded under Generals J. E. B Stuart, F. Lee, Wickham, and Munford. It participated in more than two hundred engagements, including the Seven Days' Battles and Stuart's ride around McClellan. The regiment was active in the conflicts at Gainesville, Second Manassas, Sharpsburg, Fredericksburg, Kelly's Ford, Chancellorsville, Brandy Station, Gettysburg, Bristoe Station, the Wilderness, Todd's Tavern, Spotsylvania, Bethesda Church, and Cold Harbor. Later it was involved in Early's operations in the Shenandoah Valley, the defense of Petersburg, and the Appomattox Campaign. In April 1862, it totaled 437 men, lost 8 percent of the 310 engaged at Gettysburg, and had 318 fit for duty in September 1864.

57. Pecquet du Bellet et al., *Some Prominent Virginia Families, Volume IV* (http://www. archive.org/stream/someprominentvir04pecq/someprominentvir04pecq_djvu.txt).

58. Driver, *1st Virginia Calvary*, 186.

59. Duncan, *Beleaguered Winchester*, 26. More men died of disease than from combat during the Civil War, a result of having large concentrations of men living under field conditions for extended periods at a time when comparatively little was known of sanitation.

60. Driver, *1st Virginia Calvary*, 186.

61. http://person.ancestry.com/tree/60027073/person/36121170592/facts

62. Driver, *1st Virginia Calvary*, 34.

63. Keith S. Bohannon, *Giles, Allegheny and Jackson Artillery* (Lynchburg, Virginia:
H. E. Howard Publishing Company Inc., 1990, p. 106.

64. F. T. Hambrecht and J. L. Koste, *Biographical Register of Physicians Who Served the Confederacy in a Medical Capacity* (Ancestry.com).

65. Sean M. Heuvel, compiler, *Remembering Virginia's Confederates* (Mount Pleasant, South Carolina: Arcadia Publishing, 2010), 88, and *7th Virginia Cavalry Regiment*, Richard L. Armstrong (Lynchburg, Virginia: H. E. Howard Publishing Company Inc., 1992), 112.

66. Terrence V. Murphy, *10th Virginia Infantry Regiment* (Lynchburg, Virginia: H. E. Howard Publishing Company Inc. 1989), 139.

67. Driver, *1st Virginia Cavalry*, 139, 140, and 186; *6th Virginia Cavalry*, 85 and 124; and Ancestry.com data.

68. Kenneth L. Stiles, *4th Virginia Cavalry Regiment* (Lynchburg, Virginia: H. E. Howard Publishing Company Inc., 117.

69. Jordan and Thomas, *19th Virginia Infantry Regiment*, 76, and *Index to Compiled Confederate Military Service Records*.

70. Driver, *1st Virginia Cavalry Regiment*, 186.

71. Wallace, *17th Virginia Infantry Regiment*, 119, and Ancestry.com.

72. William Cullen Sherwood, *Nelson Artillery, Lamkin and Rives Reserves* (Lynchburg, Virginia: H. E. Howard Publishing Company, 1991), 99.

73. Richard B. Kleese, *23rd Virginia Cavalry Regiment* (Lynchburg, Virginia: H. E. Howard Publishing Company Inc. 1996), 15, 43, and 68, *See also*

Cole County, Missouri, Historical Society, http://colecohistsoc.org/civil-war6.html.

74. Ibid., 68.

75. Mark A. Snell, *West Virginia and the Civil War: Mountaineers Are Always Free* (Charleston, South Carolina: The History Press, 2011), 165.

BIBLIOGRAPHY

In addition to the following works, I consulted every regimental history in The Virginia Regimental Histories Series in which Hites or Major Hite's descendants served. These are noted in appropriate footnotes for each entry.

Anthony, Arthur. *General Jo Shelby's March.* New York: Random House, 2010.

Ashby, Thomas A. *The Valley Campaign, Being the Reminiscences of a Non-Combatant between the Lines in the Shenandoah Valley During the War of the States.* New York: Neale Publishing House, 1914.

Bell, Sadie. *The Church, the State, and Education in Virginia.* Harrisonburg, Pennsylvania: Science Press Printing Company, 1930.

Bourne, Jennie, Carleton University. "Slavery in the United States," EH.net, Economic History Association, http://eh.net/encyclopedia/article/wahl.slavery.us.

Cartmell, Thomas Kemp. *Shenandoah Valley Pioneers and their Descendants: A History of Frederick County, Virginia.* Isha Books, New Delhi; 2013. Originally published by the Eddy Press Corporation in Winchester, Virginia, 1909.

Colt, Margaretta Barton. *Defend the Valley: A Shenandoah Family in the Civil War.* New York: Orion Books, 1994.

Duncan, Richard R. *Beleaguered Winchester: A Virginia Community at War, 1861–1865.* Baton Rouge: Louisiana State University Press, 2007.

Ebert, Rebecca A., and Teresa Lazazzera. *Frederick County, Virginia: From the Frontier to the Future: A Pictorial History.* Norfolk, Virginia: The Donning Company, 1988.

Harper, Bryant R. *A Factual History of Education in Winchester, Virginia.* Charlottesville: University of Virginia, unpublished thesis, October 1944.

Heinemann, Ronald L., John G. Kolp, Anthony S. Parent Jr., and William G. Shade. *Old Dominion, New Commonwealth: A History of Virginia, 1607–2007,* Charlottesville: University of Virginia Press, 2007.

Heuvel, Sean M. comp. *Remembering Virginia's Confederates.* Charleston, South Carolina: Arcadia Publishing, 2010.

Hewett, Janet B., *The Roster of Confederate Soldiers, 1861–1865,* Vol. VIII, Wilmington, North Carolina: Broadfoot Publishing Company, 1995.

Hite, Richard. *Sustainable Genealogy: Separating Fact from Fiction in Family Legends.* Baltimore, Maryland: Genealogical Publishing Company, 2013.

Hofstra, Warren R. *A Separate Place: The Formation of Clarke County, Virginia.* Madison, Wisconsin: Madison House Publishers, 1999.

Hofstra, Warren R. *The Planting of New Virginia: Settlement and Landscape in the Shenandoah Valley.* Baltimore, Maryland: The Johns Hopkins University Press, 2004.

Hofstra, Warren R. *The Great Valley Road of Virginia: Valley Landscapes from Prehistory to the Present.* Charlottesville, Virginia: University of Virginia Press, 2010.

Holsworth, Jerry W. *Civil War Winchester,* Charleston, South Carolina: The History Press, 2011.

Hutton, James V., comp. *Frederick County Census of 1850,* Athens, Georgia: Iberian Publishing Company, 1987.

BIBLIOGRAPHY

Jessup, Harlan R., ed. *The Painful News I Have to Write.* Baltimore, Maryland: Butternut and Blue Publishers, 1998.

Kercheval, Samuel. A *History of the Valley of Virginia.* Dayton, Virginia: C. J. Carrier Company, 2013. Originally published in 1833.

Mahon, Michael G. *The Shenandoah Valley, 1861–1865: The Destruction of the Granary of the Confederacy.* Harrisburg, Virginia: Stackpole Press, 1999.

Mitchell, Robert D., ed. *Appalachian Families: Settlement, Society and Development in the Pre-Industrial Era.* Lexington: University of Kentucky Press, 1990.

Norris, J. E. *History of the Lower Shenandoah Valley: Counties of Frederick, Berkeley, Jefferson, and Clarke; their Early Settlement and Progress to the Present Time; Geological Features; a Description of their Historic and Interesting Localities; Cities, Towns, and Villages.* Chicago: A. Warner and Co., 1890. Nabu Public Domain Reprints, undated.

Noyalas, Jonathan A. *Two Peoples, One Community: The African American Experience in Newtown (Stephens City), Virginia, 1850–1860.* Stephens City, Virginia: The Stone House Foundation, 2007.

Pecquet du Bellet, Louise. *Some Prominent Virginia Families.* 4 vols. Lynchburg, Virginia: J. P. Bell Company, 1907.

Quarles, Garland R. Occupied Winchester, 1861–1865. Winchester, Virginia: Winchester-Frederick County Historical Society, 1976.

Sharpe, Hal F. *Shenandoah County in the Civil War: Four Dark Years.* Charleston, South Carolina: The History Press, 2012.

Snell, Mark A. *West Virginia and the Civil War: Mountaineers Are Always Free.* Charleston, South Carolina: The History Press, 2011.

Sydnor, Charles S. *The Development of Southern Sectionalism, 1819–1848.* Baton Rouge: Louisiana State University Press, 1948.

Tragle, Henry Irving. *The Southampton Slave Revolt of 1831: A Compilation of Source Material, Including the Full Text of the Confessions of Nat Turner.* Amherst, Massachusetts: University of Massachusetts Press, 1971.

Wilkins, James Richard. *Pioneers and Patriots: A History of the John Wilkins and Some Related Families of Virginia: Tuck, Hite, Wall, Winn, and Others.* Winchester, Virginia: James R. Wilkins, 1980.

APPENDIX A

Virginia Hites Who Died Fighting for the Confederacy

Grandson: * Great-Grandson: **

This appendix includes twenty-six Hites who gave the "last full measure" fighting for the Confederacy, including four of Major Hite's grandsons and two great-grandsons. There were undoubtedly others, as Confederate records are fragmentary and there were a number of spelling variants for family members. Many Civil War casualties were buried as "unknowns," while many other remains were not recovered from the many skirmishes and battles during four years of vicious warfare. Many soldiers from both sides rest in unmarked graves.

In addition, Confederate records often simply note "mustered out" or "did not survive the war" without providing specific details regarding what actually occurred. I have reflected these notations even when actual cause of death is provided elsewhere.

Whenever possible, I attempted to associate the soldier with his parents. However, the Hite family's exponential growth and paucity of data made this impossible in most cases.

THE HITE'S CIVIL WAR

1. Cornelius Hite Davison * (see p. 30)

2. Andrew J. Hite Born about 1840, he was a farmer from News Ferry, Halifax County, and twenty-one years old when he enlisted on June 1, 1861, as a private in Company K, 20th Virginia Infantry Regiment. He was five feet nine inches tall, with a dark complexion, dark eyes, and dark hair.

Source: *The 20th, 39th, and Virginia Infantry Battalions*, George L. Sherwood Jr. and Jeffrey C. Weaver, H. E. Howard Publishing Company Inc., Lynchburg, 1994, p. 54, The Virginia Regimental Histories Series.

3. Benjamin E. Hite Born about 1837, he was a farmer from Rockbridge County, twenty-four years old when he enlisted on April 20, 1861, as a private in Company H, 4th Virginia Infantry Regiment. He was wounded at First Manassas on July 21, 1861. He later died in a Winchester hospital from a fever associated with his wound. His records noted "mustered out" December 8, 1861, at Winchester and "did not survive the war."

Source: *The 4th Virginia Infantry Regiment*, James I. Robertson, H. E. Howard Publishing Company Inc., Lynchburg, 2004, p. 56, The Virginia Regimental Histories Series.

4. David Christian Hite A farmer from Mill Creek, Page County, he was born about 1832, and married Dianah Cline about 1855. David enlisted as a private in Company H ("Page County Greys"), 33rd Virginia Infantry Regiment, part of the Stonewall Brigade, on April 22, 1862, when he was twenty-eight years old. He was wounded at Second Manassas on August 26, 1862. He was reported as present for duty the beginning of July 1863, but taken prisoner at Gettysburg on July 4, 1863. He was sent first to Baltimore and then to Point Lookout, Maryland, on August 20, 1863. He was exchanged on March 17, 1864, and was subsequently killed during the Third Battle of Winchester on September 19, 1864, when a cannon ball severed most of both legs between his body and knees. His body was never

APPENDIX A

recovered and most likely was buried in an unmarked grave. A service was held for him in Page County on September 10, 1865.

Memoritechnica.

David C. Hite departed this life September 19th 1864. He fell mortally wounded in the memorable battle at Winchester, about two hours before sundown. He was struck by a cannon ball, taking both legs neatly off between the body and the knees. Some of the company being close by, went to his aid, but found his situation such that he could not be moved and the enemy pressing very close. They told him his situation was such that he could not be moved and he told them to lay him down and do the best they could for themselves; they did so and placed his knapsack under his head and left him; that is the last we have ever heard of him. It is supposed that he bled to death in a very short time. He belonged to the 33rd Regiment Va. Volunteers, and the Stonewall Brigade. His body is now numbered among the dead, while his soul ever liveth and we hope forever at rest. He was wounded twice before, one time in the arm slightly and the next time in the neck badly. His age was 31 years 11 month and 3 days.

Memorial Notice From David Hite's Funeral Service
September 10, 1865.

David was one of four sons of Daniel and Rebecca Hite from a farm on Mill Creek in Page County who fought for the Confederacy. Two other sons died of wounds sustained in battle—Lieutenant William Francis at First Manassas and John Pendleton at Gettysburg. Only Isaac Martin Hite survived the war. See John Pendleton Hite, below, for the regiment's fate over the course of the war.

Sources: *The 33rd Virginia Infantry Regiment*, Lowell Reidenbaugh, H. E. Howard Publishing Company Inc., 1987, p. 124, The Virginia Regimental Histories Series, and *The Painful News I Have to Write: Diary of Four Hite Brothers of Page County in the Service of the Confederacy*, Army of Northern Virginia Series, Butternut and Blue, 1998, p. 166.

5. George Smith Hite * (see p. 32

6. Hugh Holmes "Scott" Hite Jr. * (see p. 33)

7. Isaac Irvine Hite Jr. ** (see p. 35)

8. Isaiah H. Hite He was from Rude's Hill in Augusta County and enlisted as a private at Charlestown, now West Virginia, on April 15, 1862, in Company G, 2nd Virginia Infantry Regiment, a part of the Stonewall Brigade. Wounded in the leg at Second Manassas on August 28, 1862, he returned to his unit on January 17, 1863. Isaiah entered Chimborazo Hospital in Richmond on December 20, 1863, suffering from catarrh (inflammation of mucous membranes in one of the airways or cavities of the body). He died at Chimborazo Hospital in Richmond of complications associated with his wounds on January 2, 1864. Records indicate "mustered out on January 2, 1864" and "did not survive the war."

Source: *The 2nd Virginia Infantry Regiment*, Dennis E. Frye, H. E. Howard Publishing Company Inc., Lynchburg, 1984, p. 105, The Virginia Regimental Histories Series.

9. James Howard Hite James was born October 8, 1844, in Red Bank, Halifax County. He was an eighteen-year-old farmer when he enlisted. According to family lore, James enlisted with his father, Spencer Perry, sometimes given with a middle initial of "T." Hite Sr. (see p. 78) and his two younger brothers, Stephen General Taylor Hite (born January 29, 1847, in Red Bank, Halifax County) and George Berryman Hite (born July 18, 1848). All except James survived the war, although no records exist for the younger brothers' service. The two would have been about fourteen and thirteen when they enlisted.

James enlisted as a private at South Boston, Halifax County, on May 14, 1861, in Company K, 14th Virginia Infantry Regiment. He was reported absent without leave on September 10, 1861, but he had returned by November 12. He was detailed as a teamster on May 13, 1862, and served in that capacity as late as January 1, 1863. Existing records reflect that he was present for roll call on March 10, 1864, and was carried on the regimental clothing list as late as November 30, 1864. Some records indicate that he died in Halifax

APPENDIX A

County in January; others report his date of death as January 11, 1864—in Warwickshire, England. Family historian James Richard Wilkins notes only that James was "killed in battle in 1864." Most genealogical records indicate that James died on January 11, 1864, during the siege of Petersburg.

This is clearly a case of faulty record keeping. There is also an individual listed as "James A. Hite" who enlisted in Richmond as a private in Company C, 2nd North Carolina Infantry Battalion, on October 19, 1861, and was captured, along with two other Hites (Edward J. and Spencer T., [his father?]) at Roanoke Island on February 8, 1862. This James was released on parole at Elizabeth City, North Carolina, February 21, 1862, and transferred to the 59th Virginia Infantry Regiment on November 15, 1862. Just to further muddy the waters, a James A. Hite is carried on Halifax County pension roles as having served in the same two units in which Spencer T. (Perry) Hite served. It is most likely that James died before Petersburg.

Sources: *The 14th Virginia Infantry Regiment*, Edward R. Crews and Timothy A. Parrish, 1995, p. 111; *59th Virginia Infantry Regiment*, George L Sherwood and Jeffrey C. Weaver, 1994, p. 149, both H. E. Howard Publishing Company Inc.,, Lynchburg, The Virginia Regimental Histories Series and *Pioneers and Patriots: A History of the John Wilkins and Some Related Families of Virginia: Tuck, Hite, Wall, Winn, and Others*. James R. Wilkins, author and publisher, 1980, p. 239.

10. James L. Hite Born about 1822, he was a farmer from Lunenburg County in Southside, Virginia, and was thirty-nine years of age on enlistment. James enlisted as a private in Company C, 20th Virginia Infantry Regiment, on May 20, 1861. The regiment participated in the battle of Rich Mountain on July 11, 1861, in Randolph County, Virginia (now West Virginia). Lieutenant Colonel John Pegram surrendered the entire regiment, so Hite was most likely imprisoned and then paroled. Confederate records indicate that he reenlisted on September 1, 1863, but was killed on August 15, 1864, in a skirmish between General Jubal Early's Army of the Valley and General Philip Sheridan's forces somewhere in the Shenandoah Valley. Confederate records simply note "mustered out; did not survive the war," supplying no other details detailing his fate.

Source: *The 20th Virginia Infantry Regiment*, George L. Sherwood and Jeffrey C. Weaver, H. E. Howard Publishing Company Inc., 1999, p. 123, The Virginia Regimental Histories Series. Wikipedia is the source of the Rich Mountain information.

11. John C. Hight (Hite) John enlisted as a private in Company B, 8th Virginia Cavalry Regiment at Wytheville, Wythe County on June 22, 1861, apparently for one year. He reenlisted June 13, 1862, at Narrows, Giles County (on New River, on the West Virginia border), July 13, 1862, but a roster notes that he returned from desertion in March without specifying the year, and was restored to duty without trial or pay "by order of Colonel Corns." He subsequently appears on a roster as deceased, no date specified.

A John Hite was shot as a deserter at Norwell House and died at Christian's Hospital, most likely this individual. He was buried in Lynchburg's Old City Cemetery on January 6, 1864. It is likely that this individual was John C. Hite.

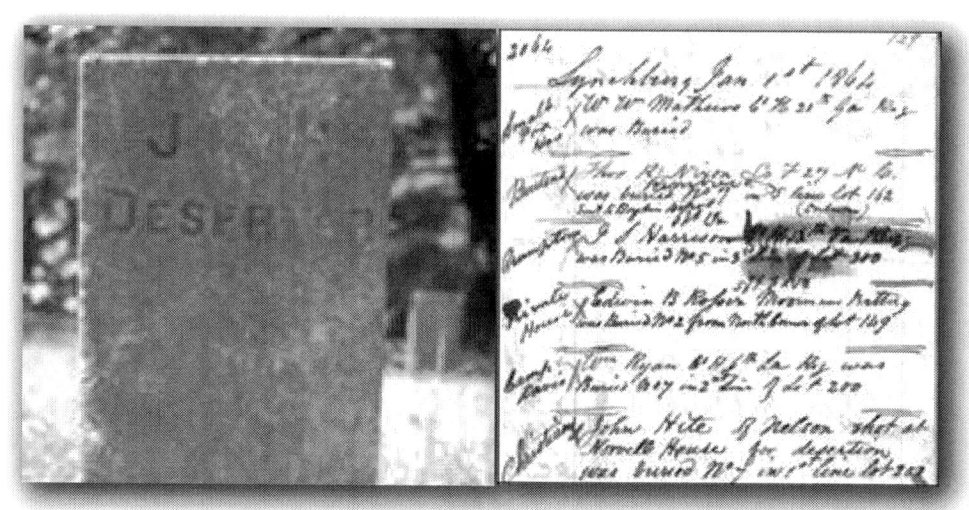

Note John Hite's tombstone with "deserter" designation above. Text of the bottom entry: "John Hite of Nelson (County) shot at Norvell House for desertion was buried No 7 in 1st line lot 202." The annotation "Christian" indicates that Hite died at Christian's Hospital.

APPENDIX A

Sources: *8th Virginia Cavalry Regiment*, Jack L. Dickinson, H. E. Howard Publishing Company Inc., 1986, p. 89, The Virginia Regimental Histories Series; e-mail from the administrative and accounting manager of Lynchburg's Old City Cemetery, July 27, 2015; www.gravegarden.org/diuguid/details.php?id= SB0112906.

12. John Henry Hite He was born about 1840 in Barbour County and was about twenty-one years old when he enlisted as a private on May 20, 1861, in Company I, 14th Virginia Cavalry Regiment. He was promoted to corporal September 15, 1862; to first sergeant on April 9, 1863, and elected "3d lieutenant" on April 1, 1864. He was accidentally wounded on August 28, 1864, and died of his wound on September 3, 1864, at York Hospital in Winchester. He is buried in St James Methodist Church Cemetery in Churchville, Augusta County.

In the course of the war's four years, 2,209 men served in the 14th Virginia Cavalry. Regimental strength fluctuated widely. All told, the regiment suffered 78 killed, 215 wounded, 330 taken prisoner, 126 who died of disease, 330 POWs—among whom 53 died while incarcerated—180 deserters, 442 transferred to other units, and 133 discharged for a variety of reasons. In January 1864, the regiment had twenty-nine officers and 424 men present for duty. By October, regimental strength was down to sixteen officers and 259 troopers. In the spring of 1865, fewer than 40 percent of the unit's men returned from furlough after being sent home to provide forage for their horses. Only thirty-four members surrendered at Appomattox.

Sources: *14th Virginia Cavalry Regiment*, Robert J. Driver Jr., H. E. Howard Publishing Company Inc.,, Lynchburg, 1988, p. 135, The Virginia Regimental Histories Series and http://www.14thvirginiacavalry.org/regiment_history.htm.

13. John M. Hite John enlisted at Harrisonburg as a private in Company G, 10th Virginia Infantry Regiment on April 18, 1861, and deserted in June 1862. Another John M. Hite, possibly the same man, served in Captain Donald's

Light Artillery Company. Hite died on May 22, 1864, and is buried in the Hite cemetery off Route 685, west of Edinburg. It is possible that he was shot as a deserter—note the similarity of the stone on the right to John C. Hight/Hite's tombstone (#11).

Source: *The 10th Virginia Infantry Regiment*, Terrence V. Murphy, H. E. Howard Publishing Company Inc.,, Lynchburg, The Virginia Regimental Histories, 1989, p. 155, Film No: M382 roll 27, Fold3.com and Ancestry.com.

14. John Pendleton Hite He was born about 1841 on a farm on Mill Creek in Page County, two miles southwest of Luray. John was one of four sons of Daniel and Rebecca Hite who fought for the Confederacy. His brother, First Lieutenant William Francis Hite, died of wounds sustained at First Manassas, and David Christian was killed during the Third Battle of Winchester. Only the fourth brother, Isaac Martin Hite, survived the war.

APPENDIX A

Sergeant John Pendleton Hite

John enlisted as a private on June 1, 1861, in Company H (the Page County Greys) of the 33rd Virginia Infantry Regiment, a part of the storied Stonewall Brigade. Because of his performance in the field, he was promoted to first sergeant. John perished from wounds sustained at Gettysburg. His regiment was part of General Richard Stoddert Ewell's 2nd Corps, which suffered tremendous losses in its attacks on the northeastern part of the Union fishhook. Only ninety soldiers from the entire regiment survived the war. The regimental history notes that Hite was left on the battlefield, "mustered out" on July 5, 1863, and "did not survive the war." Evidently there is more to John's story, since he is buried in Hollywood Cemetery in Richmond. Very likely his body was exhumed some years after the war and buried along with other Confederate dead by the Daughters of the Confederacy.

John left an extensive diary of a soldier's life in the field, *The Painful News I Have to Write*. He was ultimately buried in Richmond's Hollywood Cemetery even though a service was held for him in Page County on September 10, 1865. A furlough pass indicates that John was five feet five of "tolerably fair" complexion, with blue eyes and light hair.

> ## Memoritechnica.
>
> —:o:—
>
> JOHN P. HITE departed this life July 4th, 1863. He fell mortally wounded on the 3rd, in the morning before sunrise and died the next morning about six o'clock. He was shot in making a charge up a steep mountain, and exposed to two fires, one in front and one from the right flank; it is supposed he was shot from the right flank; he was struck in the right shoulder, the ball ranged downward, passed through near the heart and lodged in the left flank just under the skin He was sensible of his situation and prayed for death, that he might be released from his suffering, about night he fell into a stupor and became unconscious and died the next morning. His age was 22 years 7 months and 20 days; he was a member of the 33rd Regiment Va. Volunteers, and belonged to the Stonewall Brigade. He fell in the memorable Battle fought at Gettysburg Pa., he was buried by his brother David, two miles north of Gettysburg. There he lies slumbering in his mother dust till Gabriel's trumpet shall bid it rise.
>
> **Memorial Notice From John Hite's Funeral Service
> September 10, 1865.**

Sources: *The 33rd Virginia Infantry Regiment*, Lowell Reidenbaugh, H. E. Howard Publishing Company Inc.,, Lynchburg, 1987, p. 124, The Virginia Regimental Histories Series, and *The Painful News I Have to Write: Diary of Four Hite Brothers of Page County in the Service of the Confederacy*, Army of Northern Virginia Series, Butternut and Blue, 1998, p. 63.

15. John S. Hite, He was born February 11, 1818, at Peaked Mount Church, Rockingham County. He was a farmer and a resident of Gilmer County, enlisting at Monterey, Highland County, as a private in Company C, 14th Virginia Cavalry Regiment, on March 11, 1862, when he was forty-four years old. Records indicate that he "reenlisted" in Churchville on May 15, 1862. He was absent without leave the last two weeks of 1862. John was captured in

APPENDIX A

Greenbrier County, sent to Wheeling, West Virginia, and forwarded first to Camp Chase and then to North Alton Prison, Illinois, where he died of gastritis on February 5, 1863. Confederate records indicate that he was "mustered out" on that date. He left his wife, Rachel, ten children to raise. He is buried in North Alton's Confederate Cemetery. He had a dark complexion, brown eyes, black hair, and stood five feet ten.

Source: *The 14th Virginia Cavalry Regiment*, Robert J. Driver Jr., H. E. Howard Publishing Company, Lynchburg, 1988, p. 135, The Virginia Regimental Histories Series.

16. John S. Hite He was born about 1818 in Monterey, Highland County. He was a resident of Gilmer County when he entered the Confederate army.

John enlisted as a private in Company C, 14th Virginia Cavalry Regiment, on March 10, 1862, when he was forty-four years old. He "reenlisted" at Churchville on May 15, 1862, was captured at Greenbrier on November 26, 1862, and sent to Wheeling, (West) Virginia. Then he was transferred to Camp Chase and Alton, Illinois. "Mustered out" on February 5, 1863, at Alton, Illinois, a Union prison, where he died of gastritis. He is buried in the North Alton Confederate Cemetery.

Source: The 14th Virginia Cavalry Regiment, H. E. Howard Publishing Company Inc.,, Lynchburg, 1988, p. 135, The Virginia Regimental Histories Series.

17. John T. Hite was born about 1838, a farmer from Lynchburg County, and about age twenty-three when he enlisted as a private in Company F of the 11th Virginia Infantry Regiment on May 29, 1861. His death may have been connected with Major General Robert F. Hoke's campaign against and capture of Forts Comfort and Williams at Suffolk, Washington County, North Carolina, in the spring of 1864. He was "mustered out" on January 15, 1864, and "did not survive the war."

Source: *The 11th Virginia Infantry Regiment*, Robert T. Bell, H. E. Howard Publishing Company Inc.,, Lynchburg, 1985, p. 79, The Virginia Regimental Histories Series.

18. Langford Hite, He was from Jackson River Depot, Allegheny County, and enlisted as a private in Company F, 60th Virginia Infantry Regiment (part of ex-Governor Wise's "Legion") on March 19, 1862, at the Jackson River Depot. He deserted on September 1, 1862, but rejoined his unit on October 5, 1862. He was under arrest in October 1863. He died of disease at Narrows, Giles County, on March 6, 1864, listed as "mustered out."

Source: *The 60th Virginia Infantry Regiment, Johnny Lee Scott*, H. E. Howard Publishing Company Inc.,, Lynchburg, 1997, p. 106, The Virginia Regimental Histories Series.

19. Nathaniel Wilson Hite He was from Fairfield, Augusta County, and enlisted as a private on July 10, 1861, in the Rockbridge Light Artillery Battery. He died of typhoid in a Confederate hospital in Gordonsville on March 1, 1863, after a three-month illness.

Source: *Rockbridge Light Artillery*, Robert J. Driver Jr., H. E. Howard Publishing Company, Lynchburg, 1987, p. 129, The Virginia Regimental Histories Series.

20. Samuel Hite He was born about 1824, and worked as a farmhand at Fairfield, Augusta County. He was thirty-seven when he enlisted as a private in the 2nd Battery, Rockbridge Light Artillery on July 10, 1861. He was reported as detailed to Staunton from July to November 1861 but died of unspecified disease on April 13, 1862. He is buried in Thornrose Cemetery in Staunton.

Another Samuel Hite with the same personal description is said to have enlisted on the same date into Company B, 52nd Virginia Infantry Regiment but as "detailed in Staunton when transferred on September 28, 1861," presumably to the artillery.

APPENDIX A

Source: *Rockbridge Light Artillery*, Robert J. Driver Jr., 1987, p. 129 and *The 52nd Virginia Infantry Regiment*, Robert J. Drover Jr., 1986, p. 121, H. E. Howard Publishing Company Inc.,, Lynchburg, The Virginia Regimental Histories Series, and material from Ancestry.com.

21. Thomas G. Hite (Military records give his middle initial as "G," although his tombstone has "J.") He was born March 10, 1843, in Front Royal, Warren County, the son of Philip Hite. Thomas was sixteen years old and a nurseryman and student when he enlisted at Front Royal as a private in the Winchester Light Artillery, Cutshaw's Battery, on March 11, 1862. He was transferred out of the battery on September 23, 1862, to the Virginia Alleghany Light Artillery of Braxton's Brigade Artillery, 2nd Corps, Army of Northern Virginia. Captain Wilfred E. Cutshaw raised the Jackson Artillery in Frederick County, Virginia, in mid-March 1862. During its brief existence, the battery (also known as the Jackson Artillery) participated in the 1862 Valley Campaign, the Seven Days' fighting (Peninsula Campaign), and the Maryland Campaign. Following Antietam (or Sharpsburg), remnants of the battery were transferred to Carpenter's Company, Virginia, Alleghany Light Artillery ("Alleghany Roughs" Artillery) on September 23, 1862, because of the unit's depleted condition. Thomas was killed in action on May 12, 1864, at Spotsylvania Court House when he was twenty-one years, two months, and two days old. His is buried in the Virginia section of the Spotsylvania Confederate Cemetery.

Source: The Giles, Allegheny, and Jackson Artillery; Keith S. Bohannon; *Winchester Light Artillery, Cutshaw's Battery*, H. E. Howard Publishing Company Inc.,, Lynchburg, 1990, pp. 106 and 115, The Virginia Regimental Histories Series.

22. Thornton Fontaine "Frank" Hite (See p. 34)*

23. William A. Hite He was born in Lexington about 1834 and enlisted as a private in Company H, 27th Virginia Infantry Regiment (the Stonewall Brigade), on July 31, 1861, at twenty-seven years of age. William was detailed as a teamster from September 5 to October 31, 1861. William died of fever (described as "mustered out") on December 15, 1861, in Winchester and is buried in Winchester's Mount Hebron's Stonewall Confederate Cemetery.

Source: *The 27th Virginia Infantry Regiment*, Lowell Reidenbaugh, H. E. Howard Publishing Company Inc.,, Lynchburg, 1993, p. 151, The Virginia Regimental Histories Series.

24. William A. Hight (Hite) He was a farmer born about 1826 in Augusta County. Hite enlisted at Staunton as a private on March 14, 1862, in Company E, 5th Virginia Infantry Regiment. He was wounded September 17, 1862, and returned to his unit in October. He was detailed to arrest deserters in early 1863. He was sent to Hamilton's Crossing hospital May 29, 1863, returning in October. He was killed during the Battle at Monocacy on July 9, 1864.

Source: *The 5th Virginia Infantry Regiment*, Lee A. Wallace Jr., H. E. Howard Publishing Company Inc.,, Lynchburg, 1988, p. 128, The Virginia Regimental Histories Series.

25. William E. Hite William enlisted in Richmond as a private in Company B, 3rd Virginia Cavalry Regiment on January 25, 1864, and was killed during the major cavalry engagement at Haws Shop on May 28, 1864. Fragmentary records suggest that he may have been drafted.

APPENDIX A

Source: *3rd Virginia Infantry Regiment*, Thomas P. Nanzig, H. E. Howard Publishing Company Inc.,, Lynchburg, 1989, p. 112, The Virginia Regimental Histories Series.

26. William Francis Hite He was born on November 14, 1840, in Page County. He was one of four sons of Daniel and Rebecca Hite who fought for the South. William enlisted in Company H ("Page County Greys"), 33rd Virginia Infantry Regiment (part of the Stonewall Brigade), as a first lieutenant—the *only* Hite who enlisted as an officer—on June 1, 1861. He was wounded during the First Battle of Manassas and died on November 17, 1861, of typhoid fever at age twenty-three. His brother, John P. Hite, who left an extensive diary of his experiences in the field, served in the same company. Their brothers, David and Isaac, also served. Only Isaac survived the war.

Sources: *The 33rd Virginia Infantry Regiment*, Lowell Reidenbaugh, H. E. Howard Publishing Company Inc.,, Lynchburg, 1987, p. 124, The Virginia Regimental Histories Series and *The Painful News I Have to Write: Diary of Four Hite Brothers of Page County in the Service of the Confederacy*, Army of Northern Virginia Series, Butternut and Blue, Baltimore, 1998.

27. William Henry Harrison Hite William was born July 27, 1840, in Augusta County and was a farm hand by occupation. William enlisted at Staunton, Augusta County, as a private in Company I, 14th Virginia Cavalry Regiment on May 13, 1861. He was captured on April 25, 1862, while scouting near Jennings Gap, Augusta County, a pass leading from West Virginia to Staunton, and sent to Camp Chase, Ohio. After being exchanged on August 25, 1862, he was sent to a hospital in Richmond. Private Hite died of chronic diarrhea, contracted during his year in captivity, at his parents' home near Jennings Gap on November 15, 1862. Records reflect this fact as "mustered out on November 15, 1862, at Jennings Gap." His brother, John Rankin Hite, became a millionaire during the gold rush of 1851.

Source: *The 14th Virginia Cavalry Regiment*, Robert J. Driver Jr., H. E. Howard Publishing Company Inc.,, Lynchburg, 1988, p. 135, The Virginia Regimental Histories Series.

28. William Meade Hite * *(See p. 36)

APPENDIX B

The Survivors

Nine of Major Hite's grandsons and a great-grandson fought for the Confederacy and survived the Civil War, as well as fifty-one other Hites. The total number of Hites from Virginia who donned the gray (or butternut) was just over one hundred men who enlisted or were conscripted into Virginia's infantry, cavalry, artillery, and engineer units

Grandson: * Great-grandson: **

1. Dr. Robert Stuart Baldwin * (see p. 39)

2. Isaac Hite Bird * (see p. 40)

3. Sgt. Mark Bird Jr. * (see p. 41)

4. A. Hite He enlisted as a private on June 25, or July 1, 1863, in Company D, 21st Virginia Cavalry Regiment. He deserted on February 3, 1864. No further information survives.

Source: *The 21st Virginia Cavalry Regiment,* John E. Olson, H. E. Howard Publishing Company Inc.,, Lynchburg, 1989, p. 69, The Virginia Regimental Histories Series.

5. Allen Hite He was born about 1825 and was a farmer from Monterey in Highland County. He was thirty-six years old when he enlisted on May 11, 1861, as a private in Company E, 31st Virginia Infantry Regiment. He was mustered out on January 1, 1863, no cause given. He was six feet tall with light complexion, blue eyes, and light hair.

Source: *The 31st Virginia Infantry Regiment,* John M. Ashcraft Jr. H. E. Howard Publishing Company Inc.,, Lynchburg, 1988, p. 132, The Virginia Regimental Histories Series.

6. Ambrose Martin Hite Ambrose was born January 31, 1843, in Page County, the son of Abraham and Ann Hite. He enlisted as a private in Company H, 33rd Virginia Infantry Regiment, on April 8, 1862. Before the war broke out, he served in Company E, 97th Virginia Militia. He was a farmer from the Marksville District of Page County.

Ambrose wrote a letter to his father, Abraham, on July 21, 1861, immediately after the battle of Manassas. Apparently, at that time he was still serving in a militia company in Winchester, part of the 7th Militia Brigade, left behind to screen the Valley from General Patterson's opposing Union forces, permitting General Joseph Johnston and his subordinate, Stonewall Jackson, to reinforce General Beauregard's troops. Ambrose's letters provide an insight into the rumor mill prevalent in most military units—he told his father that the rebels had killed eight thousand to ten thousand "northerns" while putting southern casualties at 700 men. According to The Civil War Trust, the Union lost 460 killed in action, 1,124 wounded, and 1,312 missing or captured (total casualties 2,896). The South lost 387 killed, 1,582 wounded, and 13 missing (total casualties 1,952) in the war's first major bloody encounter.

APPENDIX B

As one would expect, Ambrose asked his father to send cheese, rolls, and butter, as well as ham. Evidently he had not taken to army chow, although he boasted that he had gotten used to "sleeping on the soft side of a plank" and had learned the soldier's knack of sleeping anytime, in any position. Ambrose also mentions that a rash of measles was going around the camps and that the men of neighboring Rockingham County were "going home by droves."

Ambrose was absent because of sickness through October 1862; he returned for duty in December 1863. He was captured on May 12, 1864, at Spotsylvania Court House, sent to Fort Delaware, and released after the close of hostilities on June 20, 1865. He taught school and was a farmer after the war, marrying Mary Cassie Brubaker in November 1869. They had at least three children. He later married Lucy Virginia Modesit in 1888 and died in Page County on January 28, 1922. He is buried in the Hite Cemetery at Mill Creek, Leakesville, in Page County. He had a ruddy complexion, light hair, gray eyes, and stood five feet six inches tall.

Source: *The 33rd Virginia Infantry Regiment*, Lowell Reidenbaugh, H. E. Howard Publishing Company Inc., Lynchburg, 1987, p. 124, The Virginia Regimental Histories Series; Film No: M382 roll 27 and Online Catalog, Library of Virginia, Call Number 50971; manuscript letter dated July 21, 1861 (Hanley Public Library Archives), and FindaGrave.com.

7. Benjamin Lewis Hite He was born June 6, 1818, in Augusta County and was a farmer from Staunton. He died on October 8, 1896, in Greenville, Augusta County, and is buried in the Haines Chapel Cemetery in Rockbridge County. He was forty-two at the time of his enlistment at Staunton on July 16, 1861, as a private in Company I, 52nd Virginia Infantry Regiment. He was detailed as a teamster for most of 1864. No further records are available.

Source: *The 52nd Virginia Infantry Regiment*, Robert J. Driver Jr., H. E. Howard Publishing Company Inc., Lynchburg, 1986, p. 121, The Virginia Regimental Histories Series.

8. Caleb V. M. Hite (Also listed as **Eleb E. Hite**) Born in Lexington, Rockbridge County, about 1840, he was a carpenter by trade. He was twenty-one years old when he enlisted as a private in Company B, 5th Virginia Infantry Regiment on April 18, 1861, at Lexington. His entire company was transferred to the 4th and 27th Infantry. Caleb served in Company E, 27th infantry. He served as color bearer through April 1862, and then he went AWOL from June 1 to October 31, 1862. He was dropped from the rolls as a deserter on December 20, 1862, but was reported as present for duty at Belle Isle (the Confederate prison), Richmond, on February 19, 1864. The medical board ultimately declared him unfit for field duty.

Source: *The 5th Virginia Infantry Regiment*, Lee A. Wallace Jr., 1988, p. 128, and *The 27th Virginia Infantry Regiment*, Lowell Reidenbaugh, 1993, p. 151, the H. E. Howard Publishing Company Inc., Lynchburg, Virginia, The Virginia Regimental Histories Series.

9. Charles Hite He was possibly born in 1821. Fragmentary records show him as a private in Company B, 12th Virginia Cavalry Regiment. He was paroled on April 15, 1865, in Winchester. He had a light complexion, blue eyes, black hair, and stood five feet seven inches tall.

Source: *The 12th Virginia Infantry Regiment*, Dennis E. Frye, H. E. Howard Publishing Company Inc., Lynchburg, 1989, p. 112, The Virginia Regimental Histories Series.

10. Cornelius Baldwin "Nealy" Hite Jr. * (see p. 42)

11. Cornelius Randolph Hite Sr. * (see p. 43)

12. Edward Hite Edward enlisted from Richmond as a private in Company G, 59th Virginia Infantry Regiment on October 19, 1861. He "mustered out" on October 27, 1862, no cause was given or is additional information available.

APPENDIX B

Source: *The 59th Virginia Infantry Regiment*, George L. Sherwood and Jeffrey C, Weaver, H. E. Howard Publishing Company Inc.,, Lynchburg, Virginia, 1994, p. 149, The Virginia Regimental Histories Series.

13. Edward J. Hite Edward enlisted in Richmond as a private in Company C, 2nd North Carolina Infantry Battalion. on October 19, 1861. He was captured on February 8, 1862, on Roanoke Island, released on parole at Elizabeth City, North Carolina, on February 2, 1862, and discharged October 27, 1862. More than likely he had suffered from wounds or malnourishment and was no longer fit for duty. He appears on the Halifax County pension list.

Source: *The 59th Virginia Infantry Regiment*, George L. Sherwood and Jeffrey C. Weaver, H. E. Howard Publishing Company Inc.,, Lynchburg, 1987, p. 76, The Virginia Regimental Histories Series, and *The Index to Compiled Confederate Military Service Records*.

14. Edward S. Hite He was a farmer born about 1840 in South Boston in Halifax County. Edward enlisted as a private in Company K, 14th Virginia Infantry Regiment, on May 14, 1861. He was reported as sick on July 8, 1861, returned for duty on September 10, 1861, but again reported sick on December 13, 1862, in Richmond. Edward was absent without leave from April 7, 1863, to September 10, 1863. He was AWOL again from February 27, 1864, to April 20, 1864. He returned on May 10, 1864, and surrendered at Appomattox on April 9, 1865.

Source: *The* 14th Virginia Infantry Regiment, Edward R. Crews and Timothy A. Parrish, H. E. Howard Publishing Company Inc.,, Lynchburg, 1995, p. 111, The Virginia Regimental Histories Series.

15. George L. Hite He was a native of Shenandoah County. Other records indicate that he may have been from Richmond, but perhaps he was simply drafted from the capital of the Confederacy. George was drafted as a private on June 9, 1863, and served in Company F, 17th Virginia Infantry Regiment. He was captured on April 7, 1865, at Amelia Court House and sent to the federal prison camp at Point Lookout, Maryland. George was released June 13, 1865, after taking the oath of loyalty to the Union. He was admitted to a hospital in Charlottesville on June 16, with "debility." Confederate records show that he was "mustered out" on June 17, 1865.

After the war, George was admitted to the Robert E. Lee Camp Soldiers' Home in Richmond on November 17, 1898. He was discharged in April 1899 at his request, but readmitted in September 1901. He was finally committed to an asylum in April 1903. No further information.

Source: *The 17th Virginia Infantry Regiment*, Lee A. Wallace Jr., H. E. Howard Publishing Company Inc.,, Lynchburg, 1990, p. 119, The Virginia Regimental Histories Series.

16. George W. Hite He was born about 1842 in Brownsburg, Rockbridge County, and was a carpenter in Nelson County. He was nineteen years old when he enlisted at Brownsburg as a private in Company H ("the Rockbridge Guards"), 25th Virginia Infantry Regiment, on May 21, 1861. He was captured at Rich Mountain on July 15, 1861, paroled two days later, and exchanged. He was then transferred to Company E, 5th Virginia Infantry, and was captured again on May 12, 1864, at Spotsylvania Courthouse. He was imprisoned at Fort Delaware and released on April 9, 1863. He stood five feet seven inches tall and had a light complexion, gray eyes, and light hair.

Source: *The 25th Virginia Infantry Regiment*, R. L. Armstrong, and *The 5th Virginia Infantry Regiment*, Lee A. Wallace Jr., 1988, p. 128, H. E. Howard Publishing Company Inc.,, Lynchburg, The Virginia Regimental Histories Series.

17. George W. Hite George enlisted as a private in Company A, 56th Virginia Infantry Regiment on July 8, 1861, in Mecklenburg County. He was in the hospital sick with measles by July 8, 1861, and on detached service as a provost guard May 8, 1864. He was paroled at Burkesville on April 14, 1865.

APPENDIX B

Source: *The 56th Virginia Infantry Regiment*, William A. Young Jr. and Patricia C. Young, H. E. Howard Publishing Company Inc.,, Lynchburg, 1990, p. 150, The Virginia Regimental Histories Series.

18. George W. Hight (Hite) He was born about 1829, and was a farmer from Augusta County. He enlisted at Greenville, Augusta County, as a private in Company E, 5th Virginia Infantry Regiment on May 29, 1861, when he was thirty-two years. George died at seventy years at Saint Mary's Creek, Rockbridge, on May 22, 1897. He had a fair complexion, gray eyes, sandy hair, and stood five feet eight inches tall. No further information.

Source: *The 5th Virginia Infantry Regiment*, Lee A. Wallace Jr., H. E. Howard Publishing Company Inc.,, Lynchburg, 1988, p. 128, The Virginia Regimental Histories Series.

19. George W. Hight (Hite) He was born about 1842 in Brownsburg, Rockbridge County, and worked as a carpenter in Nelson County. He enlisted at Brownsburg as a private in Company H ("Rockbridge Guards"), 25th Virginia Infantry Regiment on May 4, 1861, when he was about nineteen years old. He was captured at Rich Mountain on July 15, 1861, paroled on July 17, 1861, and exchanged. He was transferred to Company E, 5th Virginia Infantry, and captured again on May 12, 1864, at Spotsylvania Court House. He was sent to Fort Delaware and released on June 20, 1865.

Source: *The 5th Virginia Infantry Regiment*, Lee A. Wallace Jr., H. E. Howard Publishing Company Inc.,, Lynchburg, 1988, p. 128, The Virginia Regimental Histories Series.

20. H. C. Hite From Halifax County, he enlisted as a private in Company H, 1st Virginia Infantry Regiment on January 23, 1863. He was wounded and captured at Gettysburg, sent to Point Lookout, and exchanged September 18, 1864. He was admitted to Chimborazo Hospital Number 1 on September 22, 1864, and was furloughed for two months.

Source: The 1st Virginia Infantry Regiment, Lee A. Wallace Jr., H. E. Howard Publishing Company Inc.,, Lynchburg, 1985, p. 98, The Virginia Regimental Histories Series.

21. Henry C. Hite He was a farmer born at Moffett's Creek in Augusta County about 1845. Henry enlisted from Orange County in Company D, 39th Virginia Cavalry Battalion (Richardson's Scouts, Guides, and Couriers), as a private on March 8, 1864. He was sick in Richmond and confined to a hospital as of August 26, 1864, and later furloughed to Augusta County. He was reported as present for duty on September 12, 1864. Henry was paroled in Stanton on May 16, 1865. Records indicate that he served as a courier for General Robert E. Lee. He was about five feet eight inches tall and had a light complexion, light hair, and blue eyes.

After the war, he lived in the Riverheads District of Augusta County, according to the 1880 census, and in 1894, he was the manufacturer and salesman for Hite's Pain Cure. He was a member of Staunton's Stonewall Jackson Camp of Confederate Veterans and was buried in his Confederate uniform in Thornrose Cemetery in Staunton after his death on November 7, 1926.

Source: *The 1st Virginia Infantry Battalion, 39th Virginia Cavalry Battalion, and 24th Virginia Partisan Ranger Battalion*, Robert J. Driver Jr. and Kevin C. Ruffner, H. E. Howard Publishing Company Inc.,, Lynchburg, 1987, p. 106, The Virginia Regimental Histories Series.

22. Henry Scott Hite He was born approximately 1825 in Nelson County and farmed in Rockbridge County, according to the 1860 census. The 1870 census carries him as a farmhand in the South River District of Rockbridge County.

Henry was conscripted as a private at New Market in Shenandoah County in Company C, 27th Virginia Infantry Regiment on April 12, 1862, when he was thirty-seven years old. Henry was "mustered out" on July 24, 1862, for

APPENDIX B

being overage, but he was again conscripted at Midway, Albemarle County, on March 21, 1864, when he was forty-four and assigned to Company E, 5th Infantry Regiment at Camp Lee in Richmond. He was seriously wounded in the right shoulder blade at Spotsylvania Court House on May 12, 1864, exposing the top of his breastbone.

After the war, he was a farmhand at Vesuvius in the South River District of Rockbridge County and received a pension in Vesuvius until his death in 1902. He had a dark complexion and blue eyes.

Source: *The 27th Virginia Infantry Regiment*, Lee A. Wallace Jr., H. E. Howard Publishing Company Inc.,, Lynchburg, Virginia, 1988, pp. 128 and 151, The Virginia Regimental Histories Series.

23. Henry T. Hite He was born about 1823 and enlisted as a private in Company C, 5th Virginia Infantry Battalion, at Fort Powhatan on May 6, 1861. He was sick in the brigade hospital by June 30, 1862, and was discharged September 23, 1862, for being over thirty-five years old. He had a fair complexion, blue eyes, light hair, and stood five feet eleven inches tall.

Source: *The 53rd Virginia Infantry Regiment and 5th Battalion Virginia Infantry*, G. Howard Gregory, H. E. Howard Publishing Company Inc.,, Lynchburg, Virginia, 1988, p. 167, The Virginia Regimental Histories Series, *The Index to Compiled Confederate Military Service Records*, and Ancestry.com.

24. Isaac Martin Hite He was born on a farm on Mill Creek, Page County, in 1835, one of four sons of Daniel and Rebecca Hite who fought for the Confederacy, and the only son who survived the war. He died in 1898.

Isaac originally served as a private in Company I, 97th Virginia Militia (or 2nd Regiment, 7th Militia Brigade) along with his cousin Isaac Hite Bird. He enlisted in Chapman's "Dixie" Light Artillery on June 6, 1861, and was promoted to corporal by the end of December. When the "Dixie" Artillery was disbanded in October 1862, he was assigned to Cayce's Artillery. In January 1863, he was assigned to Company C, 39th Battalion, Virginia Cavalry, which was part of General Lee's bodyguard. This battalion was also known as Richardson's Battalion of Scouts, Guides, and Couriers.

Isaac surrendered at Appomattox Court House on April 9, 1865, "with horse and equipments," the only son of Daniel and Rebecca Hite who survived the war. Several years later, in 1868, he married Mary Ann Gander, the sister of a comrade; they moved to Cooper, Missouri, in 1885.

Sources: *The 1st Virginia Infantry Battalion, 39th Virginia Cavalry Battalion and 24th Virginia Partisan Ranger Battalion*, Robert J. Driver Jr. and Kevin C. Ruffner, H. E. Howard Publishing Company Inc.,, 1987, p. 106, and *The Danville, Eighth Star, New Market and Dixie Artillery*, Robert H. Moore, H. E. Howard Publishing Company Inc.,, Lynchburg, The Virginia Regimental Histories Series, 1988, p. 104.

25. Isaac Williams Hite * (see p. 44)

26. Isaac H. Hite He was a farmer from Alleghany County. Isaac enlisted as a private in Company E, 31st Virginia Infantry Regiment, on March 31,

1862. He had a fair complexion, hazel eyes, brown hair, and stood five feet four inches tall. No further information is available.

Source: *The 31st Virginia Infantry Regiment*, John M. Ashcraft Jr., H. E. Howard Publishing Company Inc.,, Lynchburg, 1988, p. 132, The Virginia Regimental Histories Series.

27. James Hite He was a carpenter from Mecklenburg County. He served as a private in Company I, 38th Virginia Infantry Regiment, with no enlistment date available. He was admitted to Orange Court House General Hospital on December 6, 1861, with pleurisy. He was discharged on January 12, 1862, diagnosed with consumption. He stood six feet one inch tall and had a sallow complexion, with dark eyes and dark hair.

Source: *38th Virginia Infantry Regiment*, G. Howard Gregory, H. E. Howard Publishing Company Inc.,, Lynchburg, 1987, p. 101, The Virginia Regimental Histories Series and *The Index to Compiled Confederate Military Service Records*.

28. James H. Hite He was born about 1843, and was a farmer from South Boston, Halifax County. James enlisted as a private on April 14, 1861, at eighteen years of age in Company K, 14th Virginia Infantry Regiment.

Source: The 14th Virginia Infantry Regiment, H. E. Howard Publishing Company Inc.,, Lynchburg, 1995, p. 111, The Virginia Regimental Histories Series.

29. James H. Hite. He was born about 1843, a farmer from South Boston in Halifax County. He enlisted at South Boston as a private in Company K, 14th Virginia Infantry Regiment, on May 14, 1861. He was present for duty on November 12, 1861, but absent without leave on September 10, 1861. By November 12, 1861, he had returned and was detailed as a teamster from May 13, 1862, through March 10, 1864. He was still on the company clothing list as of November 30, 1864.

Source: *14th Virginia Infantry Regiment*, Edward R. Crews and Timothy A. Parrish,

H. E. Howard Publishing Company Inc.,, Lynchburg, 1995, p. 111, The Virginia Regimental Histories Series, and Ancestry.com.

30. James Madison Hite Jr. * (see p. 44)

31. John A. Hite He was a farmer born on April 7, 1837, in Middlebrook in Augusta County. He enlisted as a private in Company H (second organization), 27th Infantry Regiment. He was married and about twenty-five years old when he enlisted. He died November 30, 1865, likely of wounds sustained during the war.

Source: *27th Virginia Infantry Regiment*, Lowell Reidenbaugh, H. E. Howard Publishing Company Inc.,, Lynchburg, 1993, p. 151, The Virginia Regimental Histories Series.

32. John H. Hight (Hite) He was born about 1836 in Augusta County and was a blacksmith. He served as a blacksmith in Company E, 5th Virginia Infantry Regiment, enlisting when he was twenty-five. He was detailed on November 25, 1862, and captured at Fishers Hill on September 22, 1864. He was sent to Elmira, New York, and exchanged on March 10, 1865. As of 1910, he resided in Newport and was seventy-five years old.

Source: The 5th Virginia Infantry Regiment, Lee A. Wallace Jr., H. E. Howard Publishing Company Inc.,, Lynchburg, 1988, p. 128, The Virginia Regimental Histories Series.

33. John Martin Hite He was born April 29, 1839, in Fairfield, Rockbridge County. He enlisted as a private on July 10, 1861, in Company B, 54th Virginia Infantry Regiment, when he was twenty-two years old. He transferred to the 2nd Company, Rockbridge Light Artillery Battery, on September 28, 1861. He

APPENDIX B

was wounded at Gettysburg on July 3rd and wounded again in his wrist, hand, and leg at Bristoe Station on October 31, 1863. He was reported present though February 28, 1865. He died in Vesuvius, Virginia, on February 15, 1914, at age seventy-one and is buried in Mount Carmel Presbyterian Cemetery.

Source: *The 54th Virginia Infantry Regiment*, G. L. Sherwood and Jeffrey C. Weaver,

H. E. Howard Publishing Company Inc.,, Lynchburg, 1995. p. 125, The Virginia Regimental Histories Series.

34. John M. Hite. John was born April 29, 1840, in Augusta County. He served as a private (no date of enlistment given) in Company C, 39th Virginia Partisan Cavalry Battalion (Richardson's Battalion of Scouts, Guides, and Couriers), and surrendered at Appomattox Court House on April 9, 1865, "with horse and bridle." He died on August 6, 1914, and is buried in Mount Carmel Presbyterian Cemetery in Augusta County.

Source: *The 1st Virginia Infantry Battalion, 39th Virginia Cavalry Battalion, and 24th Virginia Partisan Ranger Battalion*, Robert J. Driver Jr. and Kevin C. Ruffner,

H. E. Howard Publishing Company Inc.,, 1987, p. 106, The Virginia Regimental Histories Series.

35. John T. Hite He was born about 1838 and was a farmer by occupation. Hite enlisted in Company F, 11th Virginia Infantry Regiment, on May 29, 1861, when twenty-three years old. He served until he went absent without leave in January 1864. No further record.

Source: 11th Virginia Infantry Regiment, Robert T. Bell, H. E. Howard Publishing Company Inc.,, Lynchburg, The Virginia Regimental Histories Series p. 79.

36. Joseph W. Hite He enlisted as a private on March 3, 1864, in Company E, 31st Virginia Infantry Regiment. No further information.

Source: *The 31st Virginia Infantry Regiment*, John M. Ashcraft Jr., H. E. Howard Publishing Company Inc.,, The Virginia Regimental Histories Series.

37. Kidder Meade Hite * (see p. 45)

38. Llewellyn Jones Hite Born about 1839, he was a farmer from Lunenburg County. He enlisted at Saint John's Church in Lunenburg County as "3rd corporal" in Company C, 20th Virginia Infantry Regiment, on May 20, 1861, when he was about twenty-two years old. He was taken prisoner with at least two other companies when Lieutenant Colonel John Pegram surrendered at Rich Mountain in West Virginia on July 11, 1861. Llewellyn was paroled on July 17 in Randolph County and discharged ("mustered out") on September 27, 1861. He reenlisted on January 20, 1864, serving in Company G, 9th Virginia Cavalry Regiment. He was paroled at Blackstone in Halifax County, on the Staunton River on April 17, 1865. He had a light complexion, brown hair, blue eyes, and stood five feet five inches.

Source: The 20th and 39th Virginia Infantry Regiments, G. L. Sherwood and Jeffrey C. Weaver, H. E. Howard Publishing Company Inc.,, Lynchburg, 1994, p. 54, The Virginia Regimental Histories Series.

39. Marion M. Hite He was born on November 9, 1821, in Orange County and later moved to Frederick County. Marion enlisted in Company A, 39th Virginia Partisan Cavalry Battalion (Richardson's Battalion of Scouts, Guides, and Couriers), as a private at Orange Court House on October 1, 1863, when he was forty-one years old. Marion served as a clerk at Headquarters, Army of Northern Virginia, from December 18, 1863, to September 3, 1864. He was admitted to a hospital in Richmond that October, suffering from "debilitas," being generally run-down, no doubt from poor nutrition and exposure to the elements. Marion surrendered at Appomattox Court House on April 9, 1865,

APPENDIX B

"with horse and equipments." He died February 20, 1902, in Nelson County and is buried in the Mount Paran Baptist Church cemetery.

Sources: *The 1st Virginia Infantry Battalion, 39th Virginia Cavalry Battalion and 24th Virginia Partisan Ranger Battalion*, Robert J. Driver Jr. and Kevin C. Ruffner, H. E. Howard Publishing Company Inc.,, Lynchburg, 1987, p. 106, The Virginia Regimental Histories Series; Film No: M382 roll 27, and Southern Historical Society Papers and Appomattox Paroles, Army of Northern Virginia.

40. Monroe Junius Hite He was born in Chicago, Illinois, on April 27, 1841. Monroe enlisted at Petersburg as a private in Company E, 13th Virginia Cavalry Regiment, on March 27, 1862. He was captured during the engagement at Southside Railroad on April 2, 1865, and sent to Hart's Island, New York City. He took the loyalty oath on June 21, 1865, and was released home to Prince George County. He died in Surry County on October 28, 1905.

Source: *The 13th Virginia Cavalry Regiment*, Daniel T. Balfour, H. E. Howard Publishing Company Inc.,., Lynchburg, 1986, p. 81, The Virginia Regimental Histories Series.

41. Peter Jacobson Hight (Hite) Peter was a farmer, born about 1837 in Nelson County. He enlisted as a private on April 15, 1862, in Company E, 5th Virginia Infantry Regiment, at Greenville. He was severely wounded in his leg on June 14, 1863, during the Second Battle of Winchester and was unable to return to duty. After the war, he became a member of Staunton's Stonewall Jackson Camp Number 25, Confederate Veterans, in 1907. A farmer in Nelson County, he died near Montebello on October 27, 1920, and is buried in Haines Chapel Cemetery in Rockbridge County.

Source: *5th Virginia Infantry Regiment*, Lee A. Wallace Jr., H. E. Howard Inc., Lynchburg, 1988, p.128, The Virginia Regimental Histories Series.

42. Robert Moore Hite He was born January 1, 1842, in Boydton, Mecklenburg County. Robert enlisted as a private in Company A, 3rd Virginia Cavalry Regiment, on May 14, 1861. His horse was killed at Sharpsburg on September 17, 1862; he was promoted to sergeant in July 1863 and brevetted to lieutenant in December 1864. No further military record after January 1865. He died in Petersburg on January 16, 1895.

Source: *3rd Virginia Infantry Regiment*, Thomas P. Nanzig, H. E. Howard Publishing Company Inc.,, Lynchburg, 1989, p. 112, The Virginia Regimental Histories Series, and Film No: M382 roll 27, Ancestry.com.

43. Robert N. Hite He was born about 1847 in Prince George County, near Richmond. He was an illiterate farm laborer, the son of John Hite and Eliza Anderson. He enlisted as a private in Petersburg on May 4, 1861, in Company K, 12th Virginia Infantry Regiment (Archers Rifles), but served in the Confederate navy for a period. He returned to his regiment in May 1862. In January and February 1862, he was sick and confined to a hospital. He was severely wounded in his in left wrist and hand by a shell fragment during Stonewall Jackson's advance along the Orange Turnpike at Chancellorsville on May 1, 1863. He was once again in a Richmond hospital from May to September 1863 because his hand was practically paralyzed. He was detailed to work at Tredegar Ironworks in Richmond on September 6, 1863, and deserted to federal forces at Fort Powhatan on the James River on March 10, 1865. He married Sarah J. Anderson on March 13, 1873, and died of chronic bronchitis in Petersburg on February 4, 1920.

Source: *The 12th Virginia Infantry Regiment*, William D. Henderson, H. E. Howard Publishing Company Inc.,, Lynchburg,1993, p. 130, The Virginia Regimental Histories Series.

44. Robert Steele Hight (Hite) He was born on March 2, 1831, at Saint Mary's Creek in Augusta County and resided in South River, Rockbridge County.

APPENDIX B

Although he was exempted from service (probably because of age), in March 1862, he enlisted in Company E, 5th Virginia Infantry Regiment, as a private on April 11, 1862, at Rude's Hill in Shenandoah County. He was slightly wounded in the thigh on June 27, 1862. He returned to his unit on September 3, 1862, and was wounded again in the chest on October 18, 1862, at Kearneysville. He was still in a Winchester hospital on July 27, 1863, and never returned to his company. On April 21, 1864, he was instructed to report to Mount Tory Blast Furnace and to indicate his presence to an authority in Richmond. Records described Robert as "one of the bravest and most loyal soldiers." Postwar, he was a farmer and Methodist minister in Blue Ridge and died at Fairfield on May 29, 1905. He is buried in Haines Chapel Cemetery in Rockbridge.

Source: *The 5th Virginia Infantry Regiment*, Lee A. Wallace Jr., H. E. Howard Publishing Company Inc.,, Lynchburg, 1988, p. 128, The Virginia Regimental Histories Series.

45. Samuel Hite He was born about 1824 and was a farmhand from Rockbridge County. He enlisted from Fairfield near Greenville. Samuel enlisted as a private in Company B, 52nd Virginia Infantry Regiment, on July 10, 1861, when he was about forty-one years old.

Source: *The 52nd Virginia Infantry Regiment*, H. E. Howard Publishing Company Inc.,, Lynchburg, 1986, p.121, The Virginia Regimental Histories Series.

46. Spencer T. Hite His name is also given as "Spencer Perry Hite." He was born in Halifax County on August 12, 1823. He enlisted in Richmond as a private on October 19, 1861, in Company C, 2nd North Carolina Infantry Battalion, the same day as his sons James Howard, Stephen General Taylor, and George Berryman enrolled in the battalion, according to a published family history. James (appendix A, 9) served and died at Petersburg in the waning days of the war. Stephen would have been about fifteen and George about fourteen years old, but no service records exist for either.

Spencer was captured on Roanoke Island along with many troops from the unit on February 8, 1862. They were released on parole at Elizabeth City, North Carolina, on February 21, 1862. He was subsequently transferred to Company G, 59th Virginia Infantry Regiment, on November 11, 1862, and surrendered with his company at Appomattox Court House on April 9, 1865.

He died February 26, 1900, and is buried in the Tuck-Hite-Wilkins Cemetery in Red Bank, Halifax County.

Source: 59th Virginia Infantry Regiment, George L Sherwood and Jeffrey C. Weaver,

H. E. Howard Publishing Company Inc.,, Lynchburg, 1987, p.149, The Virginia Regimental Histories Series and *Pioneers and Patriots: A History of the John Wilkins Family and Some Related Families of Virginia: TUCK-HITE-WILL-WINN, 1618–1979*, James Richard Wilkins, Winchester, 1980, p. 239.

47. Thomas C. Hite He was born about 1833 and enlisted as a private in Company C, 5th Virginia Infantry Battalion on June 6, 1862, at Fort Powhatan. He transferred to Company D, 53rd Virginia Infantry Regiment, on September 25, 1862, at Hardy's Bluff, but he was absent, sick in Richmond, from that date until October 31. He was detached for service as a cooper (barrel maker) from December 1862 to October 31, 1863. He was severely wounded in the arm at Drewry's Bluff, May 16, 1864, and deserted to Union forces at Bermuda Hundred on January 13, 1865. He took the loyalty oath and was sent to Norfolk four days later.

Source: *54th Virginia Infantry Regiment, and 5th Battalion Virginia Infantry*, G. Howard Gregory, H. E. Howard Publishing Company Inc.,, Lynchburg, 1987, pp.130 and 167, The Virginia Regimental Histories Series.

48. Thomas H. Hite, He was from Hardy's Bluff, Isle of Wright County. Thomas enlisted as a private on March 14, 1862, at Hardy's Bluff, Isle of Wright

APPENDIX B

County, and was transferred to Company D, 53rd Virginia Infantry Regiment, on September 25, 1862. He was "mustered out" on January 13, 1865, at Bermuda Hundred, probably indicating that he was either wounded or captured.

Source: *The 53rd Virginia Infantry Regiment*, H. E. Howard Publishing Company Inc.,, Lynchburg, The Virginia Regimental Histories Series, and *The Roster of Confederate Soldiers, 1861–1865, Volume VIII*, Janet B. Hewett, editor, Broadfoot Publishing Company, Wilmington, North Carolina, 1996, p. 42.

49. Walker Maury Hite Jr. * (see p. 45)

50. Walter P. Hite Born in Prince George County about 1822, he was a farmer. He enlisted as a private on May 6 or 11, 1861, in Company C, 5th Battalion Virginia Infantry, at Fort Powhatan. He was discharged at Hardy's Bluff on disability because of rheumatism. His complexion was fair, he had dark eyes and dark hair and was five feet eight inches tall.

Source: *The 653rd Virginia Cavalry Regiment and 5th Battalion Virginia Infantry*, G. Howard Gregory, H. E. Howard Publishing Company Inc.,, 1990, p. 130, The Virginia Regimental Histories Series.

51. William B. Hite He was born in Covington, Alleghany County, about 1840, a blacksmith by trade. William enlisted as a private in Company A, 27th Virginia Infantry Regiment, on April 22, 1861. Some records indicate that he served as a blacksmith in the Allegheny Light Artillery Battery. He deserted on September 16, 1861, at Camp Harman, located about a mile from Centerville.

Source: *27th Virginia Infantry Regiment*, Lowell Reidenbaugh, 1993, p. 151 and *The Giles, Alleghany and Jackson Artillery*, Keith S. Bohanan, 1990, p. 106, H. E. Howard Publishing Company Inc.,, Lynchburg, The Virginia Regimental Histories Series.

52. William Franklin Hite He was born on March 11, 1844, in Barbour County and enlisted as a private in Kanawha County (now West Virginia) in Company I, 14th Virginia Cavalry Regiment, on October 16, 1862, when he was eighteen years old. He was captured in Greenbrier County on November 26, 1862, and sent to Wheeling, then transferred to prison camps in Ohio (Camp Chase) and Alton, Illinois. He was exchanged on April 8, 1863, and served with his unit from December 1863 to mid-December 1864. He was paroled in Harrisonburg on May 23, 1865. He stood five feet nine inches tall, had a fair complexion, light hair, and blue eyes. The 1870 census listed him as a merchant in Summer Dean, Augusta County. He resided in California in 1916.

Source: *The 14th Virginia Cavalry Regiment*, Robert J Driver Jr., H. E. Howard Publishing Company Inc.,, Lynchburg, 1988, p. 135, The Virginia Regimental Histories Series.

53. William H. Hight (Hite) He was a farmer born about 1840 in Augusta County. William enlisted at Greenville as a private in Company E, 5th Virginia Infantry Regiment on April 18, 1861. He was granted a reenlistment furlough from February to April 1862, but was captured in Augusta County on April 23, 1862. He was exchanged on August 5, 1862, but was wounded on October 8, 1862, while attempting to capture deserters. He was confined to a hospital in Charlottesville on October 17, 1862. He was absent and sick for an undetermined period, returning in December 1862. He was captured on May 12, 1864, at Spotsylvania Court House and sent to Fort Delaware. He was probably exchanged, but taken prisoner again at Blacks and Whites (now Blackstone, on the North Carolina border) and sent to Camp Chase, Ohio. No date of release is given, but he is presumed to have survived the war.

Source: *The 5th Virginia Infantry Regiment*, Lee A. Wallace Jr., H. E. Howard Publishing Company Inc.,, Lynchburg, 1988, p. 128, The Virginia Regimental Histories Series.

54. William L. Hite William enlisted at Camp Lee, Richmond, as a private in Company E, 14th Virginia Infantry Regiment on September 10, 1864. He

APPENDIX B

was reported as an administrator at Chimborazo hospital on March 19, 1865. On March 23, 1865 he was transferred to Company A, 3rd Virginia Cavalry. He was paroled on May 26, 1865 in Richmond.

Source: *The 14th Virginia Infantry Regiment*, Edward R. Crews and Timothy A. Parrish, 1995, p. 111, and *The 3rd Virginia Cavalry Regiment*, Thomas P. Nanzig, 1989, p. 112, H. E. Howard Publishing Company Inc.,, Lynchburg, The Virginia Regimental Histories Series.

55. William O. Hite From Boys; no further personal information available. William enlisted as a private in Company A, 3rd Virginia Cavalry Regiment on July 25, 1861. No further record after he was reported in a hospital in May 1862.

Source: *3rd Virginia Infantry Regiment*, Thomas P. Nanzig, H. E. Howard Publishing Company Inc.,, Lynchburg, 1989, p. 112, The Virginia Regimental Histories Series.

56. William Paul Hite He was born June 19, 1845, and was a farmhand from Fairfield in Augusta County's South River District (1860 census), age fifteen or sixteen when he enlisted. There appears to be some discrepancy in the records for this individual. *The Roster of Confederate Soldiers, 1861–1865* lists three individuals named William Paul Hite. One source reports that William Paul Hite enlisted in B Company, 2nd Rockbridge Artillery Battery, on July 12, 1861, at Fairfield in Rockbridge County. There is also a suggestion that William Paul may not have been a model soldier. This service record notes "AWOL sometime after October, 1862, and fined $15." However, he was faithful until the end: he was wounded in the shoulder (his collarbone was broken in two places) at Petersburg on August 8, 1864, and captured on April 2, 1865. He was sent to Point Lookout and released on June 19, 1865, after taking the loyalty oath.

Another Regimental Historical Series record notes: "Enlisted as a private on July 12, 1861, in Company B, 52nd Virginia Infantry Regiment." Records reflect simply, "mustered out on September 28, 1861." This individual was born in 1845, was sixteen years old on enlistment, and was a farmhand from Fairfield, Rockbridge County. Many artillerymen were selected for service from infantry units. Use of "mustered out" is ambiguous in The Virginia Regimental Histories Series. It could be interpreted as "dropped from the rolls," either because of desertion, sickness, or wounds, or transferred to another unit.

William Paul had a light complexion, brown hair, and hazel eyes. He was a farmhand in Rockbridge County as of 1870. He died there on April 3, 1901, and is buried in Haines Chapel Cemetery.

Source: *The 1st and 2nd Rockbridge Artillery*, James R. Driver Jr., 1987, p. 129, and *The 52nd Virginia Infantry Regiment*, Robert J. Driver, 1986, p. 121, H. E. Howard Publishing Company Inc.,, Lynchburg, The Virginia Regimental Histories Series.

57. William Paul Hite No personal information available. He enlisted as a private in Company B, 60th Virginia Infantry Regiment, on July 1, 1861, at Gauley Bridge, now West Virginia. He was detached as a teamster on August 20, 1861, and was absent without leave on November 1, 1861. No further information available.

Source: *The 60th Virginia Infantry Regiment*, Johnny Lee Scott, H. E. Howard Publishing Company Inc.,, Lynchburg, 1987, p. 106, The Virginia Regimental Histories Series.

58. William P. Hite, He was born about 1840 in Meadow Bluff in Greenbrier County in what is now West Virginia. William enlisted as a private in Company C, 46th Virginia Infantry Regiment, on June 10, 1861. No further information available on his military service.

Source: *The 46th Virginia Infantry Regiment*, Darrell C. Collins, H. E. Howard Publishing Company Inc.,, Lynchburg, 1989, p. 98, The Virginia Regimental Histories Series.

APPENDIX B

59. William Smith Davison ** (see p. 49)

60. William S. Hite He was born in Augusta County on October 11,1829, and moved to Rockbridge County in 1854. He was a farmer from the Walker's Creek District of Rockbridge County. William enlisted as a private in Company B, 27th Virginia Infantry Regiment, part of the Stonewall Brigade, on March 19, 1862, when he was approximately thirty-two years of age. Hite was captured at First Winchester on November 11, 1862, sent to Fort Delaware, and paroled on August 5,1862. When he returned to his unit, he was discharged on August 15 as being overage, but as Southern manpower waned, he was conscripted in February 1863. He was wounded in the shoulder at Gettysburg on July 3, 1863, during Pickett's Charge and imprisoned at David's Island, New York. He was exchanged on September 16, 1864, after which there is no further record. It is possible that he simply elected to go home or was no longer fit for duty. William died on October 4, 1885; he is buried in Mount Hermon Lutheran Cemetery in Newport, Augusta County.

Source: *27th Virginia Infantry Regiment*, Lowell Reidenbaugh, H. E. Howard Publishing Company Inc.,, Lynchburg,1993, p. 151, The Virginia Regimental Histories Series.

61. W. L. Hite No personal information available. Hite served as a private in Company A, 3rd Virginia Cavalry Regiment—no enlistment date given. He was paroled after hostilities ended on May 25, 1865, apparently in Richmond.

Source: *The 3rd Virginia Infantry Regiment*, Thomas P. Nanzig, H. E. Howard Publishing Company Inc.,, Lynchburg, 1989, p. 112, The Virginia Regimental Histories Series.

Appendix C

Ancestry.com Roster of Civil War Hites

Confederate

Name	Unit	State
A. L. Hite	67th Tennessee Cavalry Regiment (Wheeler's)	Tennessee
Albert Hite	13th South Carolina Infantry Regiment	South Carolina
Alfred Hite	40th Georgia Infantry Regiment	Georgia
Andrew J. Hite	11th Georgia Infantry Regiment	Georgia
C. M. Hite	Greenleaf's Company, Orleans Light Horse Cavalry	Louisiana
C. M. Hite	5th Louisiana Infantry Regiment	Louisiana
D. W. Hite	7th South Carolina Infantry Regiment	South Carolina
Edward Hite	2nd North Carolina Infantry Battalion	North Carolina
F. A. Hite	21st/22nd Tennessee Consolidated Cavalry Regiment	Tennessee
F. A. Hite	21st Tennessee Cavalry Regiment (Wilson's)	Tennessee
Francis A. Hite	1st Tennessee Infantry Regiment (Field's)	Tennessee
George D. Hite	Louisiana Confederate Guards Regiment	Louisiana
George Hite	16th Missouri Infantry Regiment	Missouri
H. B. Hite	13th Regiment, Texas Volunteers	Texas
H. H. Hite	Yeager's Regiment, Mississippi Cavalry	Mississippi
Henry D. Hite	5th Kentucky Mounted Infantry Regiment	Kentucky
Henry Hite	1st Arkansas Cavalry Regiment	Arkansas
Henry T. Hite	5th Battalion, Virginia Infantry	Virginia
Hugh S. Hite	17th Virginia Infantry Regiment	Virginia
Irvin J. Hite	1st Virginia Cavalry Regiment	Virginia
Irvin L. Hite	1st Virginia Cavalry Regiment	Virginia
Isaac H. Hite	31st Virginia Infantry Regiment	Virginia
Isaac N. Hite	39th Virginia Cavalry Battalion	Virginia
Isaac W. Hite	19th Virginia Infantry Regiment	Virginia

APPENDIX C

Isaiah H. Hite	2nd Virginia Infantry Regiment	Virginia
J. A. Hite	1st Alabama Reserve Regt (62nd Infantry Regiment)	Alabama
J. C. Hite	2nd Tennessee Cavalry Regiment	Tennessee
J. F. Hite	6th Virginia Cavalry Regiment	Virginia
J. Fontaine Hite	1st Virginia Cavalry Regiment	Virginia
J. Hite	2nd Regiment, SC State Troops (6 months, 1863–4)	South Carolina
J. J. Hite	122nd Virginia Militia Regiment	Virginia
J. J. Hite	11th Georgia Infantry Regiment	Georgia
J. J. Hite	30th North Carolina Infantry Regiment	North Carolina
J. L. Hite	9th Virginia Cavalry Regiment (Johnson's)	Virginia
J. L. Hite	9th Tennessee Cavalry Regiment (Ward's)	Tennessee
J. S. Hite	21st Virginia Cavalry Regiment	Virginia
J. S. Hite	46th Virginia Infantry Regiment	Virginia
J. T. Hite	2nd Battalion, Kentucky Mounted Rifles	Kentucky
J. W. Hite	41st Virginia Cavalry Battalion (White's)	Virginia
J. W. Hite	4th Kentucky Mounted Rifle Infantry Regiment	Kentucky
Jackson Hite	67th Virginia Militia Regiment	Virginia
Jackson Hite	60th Tennessee Mounted Inf Regiment (Crawford's)	Tennessee
Jacob Hite	52nd Georgia Infantry Regiment	Georgia
Jacob W. Hite	60th Tennessee Mounted Inf Regiment (Crawford's)	Tennessee
James A. Hite	58th Virginia Infantry Regiment	Virginia
James a. Hite	2nd Battalion, North Carolina Infantry	North Carolina
James H. Hite	14th Virginia Infantry Regiment	Virginia
James H. Hite	18th Virginia Heavy Artillery Battalion	Virginia
James Hite	Wright's Company, Halifax Heavy Artillery	Virginia
James Hite	38th Virginia Infantry Regiment (Pittsylvania)	Virginia
James Hite	26th Georgia Infantry Regiment	Georgia
James Hite	26th Georgia Infantry Regiment	Georgia
James Hite	29th Alabama Infantry Regiment	Alabama
James Hite	10th Tennessee Cavalry Regiment (DeMoss's)	Tennessee
James L. Hite	20th Virginia Infantry Regiment	Virginia

James M. Hite	33rd Georgia Infantry Regiment	Georgia
John C. Hite	Gregory's Company, High Hill Grey Virginia Infantry	Virginia
John C. Hite	34th Virginia Infantry Regiment	Virginia
John Henry Hite	14th Virginia Cavalry Regiment	Virginia
John Hite	22nd Virginia Cav Regt (Bowen's Mounted Riflemen)	Virginia
John Hite	6th VA Local Def Bn (Tredegar factory defense)	Virginia
John Hite	4th Kentucky Mounted Rifle Infantry Regiment	Kentucky
John N. Hite	5th Virginia Infantry Regiment	Virginia
John P. Hite	33rd Virginia Infantry Regiment	Virginia
John S. Hite	14th Virginia Cavalry Regiment	Virginia
John S. Hite	14th Virginia Cavalry Regiment	Virginia
John T. Hite	11th Virginia Infantry Regiment	Virginia
Joseph Hite	20th South Carolina Infantry Regiment	South Carolina
Joseph Hite	1st SC Inf Regt (McCreary's 1st Provisional Army)	South Carolina
Josiah Hite	17th Virginia Infantry Regiment	Virginia
L. Hite	22nd Battalion, Georgia Heavy Artillery	Georgia
L. Hite	47th North Carolina Infantry Regiment	North Carolina
I. J. Hite	9th Virginia Cavalry Regiment (Johnson's)	Virginia
Langford Hite	60th VA Infantry Regiment (3rd Regt, Wise's Legion)	Virginia
Llewellyn Hite	20th Virginia Infantry Regiment	Virginia
Madison J. Hite	1st Virginia Cavalry Regiment	Virginia
Martin Hite	97th Virginia Militia Regiment (Spitler's)	Virginia
Monroe J. Hite	13th Virginia Cavalry Regiment (12 months, 1861–2)	Virginia
N. W. Hite	15th South Carolina Infantry Regiment	South Carolina
Nathaniel W.	Donald's Company, Virginia Light Artillery	Virginia
Nicholas Hite	Washington County Virginia Militia	Virginia
P. S. Hite	6th Battalion, Virginia Reserves	Virginia
Patrick H. Hite	Hounsells's Battalion, VA Cavalry (Partisans)	Virginia
Patrick H. Hite	Thurmond's Company, VA Cavalry (Partisans)	Virginia
Patrick Hite	13th South Carolina Infantry Regiment	South Carolina
R. N. Hite	6th Battalion, Virginia Inf, Local Def (Tredegar Bn)	Virginia

APPENDIX C

Randal O. Hite	4th Virginia Cavalry Regiment	Virginia
Randolph Hite	4th Virginia Cavalry Regiment	Virginia
Robert A. Hite	12th Virginia Infantry Regiment	Virginia
Robert N. Hite	12th Virginia Infantry Regiment	Virginia
S. T. Hite	59th Virginia Infantry Regiment	Virginia
Samuel P. Hite	5th Virginia Infantry Regiment	Virginia
Spencer Hite	14th Virginia Infantry Regiment	Virginia
Spencer Hite	59th Virginia Infantry Regiment	Virginia
Spenser Hite	2nd Battalion, North Carolina Infantry	North Carolina
Stanmon Hite	Walker's Battalion, South Carolina Infantry	South Carolina
Stanmore Hite	19th South Carolina Infantry Regiment	South Carolina
T. S. Hite	44th Georgia Infantry Regiment	Georgia
Th. H. Hite	6th Battalion VA Local Defense Infantry (Tredegar)	Virginia
Thomas H. Hite	5th Battalion, Virginia Infantry	Virginia
Thomas H. Hite	53rd Virginia Infantry Regiment	Virginia
Thomas Hite	Gregory's Company, High Hill Greys Infantry	Virginia
Thomas Hite	2nd Virginia Infantry Regiment, Local Defense	Virginia
Thomas Hite	2nd Bn, VA Inf Local Def (Waller's Quartermasters)	Virginia
Thomas Hite	38th Virginia Infantry Regiment (Pittsylvania)	Virginia
Thomas J. Hite	Cutshaw's (Jackson's) Company, Virginia Lt Artillery	Virginia
Thomas J. Hite	51st Virginia Militia Regiment	Virginia
W. B. Hite	Walker's Battalion, South Carolina Infantry	South Carolina
W. J. Hite	1st Regiment, Virginia Reserves (Faimholt's)	Virginia
W. L. Hite	3rd Virginia Cavalry Regiment	Virginia
W. M. Hite	2nd Mississippi State Cavalry Regiment	Mississippi
Walter P. Hite	5th Battalion, Virginia Infantry	Virginia
William A. Hite	27th Virginia Infantry Regiment	Virginia
William B. Hite	27th Virginia Infantry Regiment	Virginia
William B. Hite	19th South Carolina Infantry Regiment	South Carolina
William C. Hite	1st Virginia Infantry Regiment (Williams Rifles)	Virginia
William E. Hite	3rd Virginia Infantry Regiment	Virginia

William F. Hite	33rd Virginia Infantry Regiment	Virginia
William F. Hite	14th Virginia Infantry Regiment	Virginia
William H. Hite	14th Virginia Cavalry Regiment	Virginia
William H. Hite	5th Virginia Infantry Regiment	Virginia
William Hite	Carpenter's Battery, Allegheny Roughs Light Artillery	Virginia
William Hite	1st Virginia Infantry Regiment (Williams Rifles)	Virginia
William Hite	45th Virginia Infantry Regiment	Virginia
William Hite	18th Georgia Infantry Regiment	Georgia
William L. Hite	14th Virginia Infantry Regiment	Virginia
William O. Hite	3rd Virginia Cavalry Regiment	Virginia
Wm. Paul Hite	Donald's Company, Virginia Light Artillery	Virginia
Wm. Paul Hite	46th Virginia Infantry Regiment	Virginia
William R. Hite	52nd Georgia Infantry Regiment	Georgia
William S. Hite	27th Virginia Infantry Regiment	Virginia
Wyatt Hite	18th Georgia Infantry Regiment	Georgia

Union

Abraham Hite	78th Illinois Infantry Regiment	Illinois
Abraham L. Hite	78th Illinois Infantry Regiment	Illinois
Abram Hite	100th Indiana Volunteer Infantry Regiment	Indiana
Albert Hite	23rd Indiana Volunteer Infantry Regiment	Indiana
Alexander Hite	30th Penn Militia Regt (mobilized for Gettysburg)	Pennsylvania
Alex. M. Hite	13th Indiana Cavalry Regiment	Indiana
Andrew H. Hite	1st Pennsylvania Lt Arty Regiment (14th Reserves)	Pennsylvania
Andrew Hite	111th Illinois Volunteer Infantry Regiment	Illinois
Andrew J. Hite	38th Indiana Volunteer Infantry Regiment	Indiana
Andrew J. Hite	37th Indiana Volunteer Infantry Regiment	Indiana
Andrew J. Hite	14th Kentucky Volunteer Infantry Regiment	Kentucky
Andrew K. Hite	136th Indiana Vol Inf Regiment (100 days, 1864)	Indiana

APPENDIX C

Andrew K. Hite	140th Indiana Volunteer Infantry Regiment	Indiana
Andrew R. Hite	140th Indiana Volunteer Infantry Regiment	Indiana
Ashbel Hite	1st West Virginia Cavalry Regiment	West Virginia
David C. Hite	153rd Indiana Volunteer Infantry Regiment	Indiana
David Hite	200th Pennsylvania Volunteer Infantry Regiment	Pennsylvania
Edward T. Hite	71st Pennsylvania Volunteer Infantry Regiment	Pennsylvania
F. Fazel Hite	12th Indiana Volunteer Infantry Regiment	Indiana
Franklin Hite	9th West Virginia Volunteer Infantry Regiment	West Virginia
Franklin Hite	2nd Maryland Inf Regiment, Potomac Home Guard	Maryland
Fridolin Hite	72nd Ohio Volunteer Infantry Regiment	Ohio
George F. Hite	2nd Maryland Inf Regiment, Potomac Home Guard	Maryland
George H. Hite	2nd Maryland Inf Regiment, Potomac Home Guard	Maryland
George Hite	16th Ohio Volunteer Infantry Regiment	Ohio
George Hite	5th Ohio Volunteer Cavalry Regiment	Ohio
George Hite	87th Pennsylvania Volunteer Infantry Regiment	Pennsylvania
George Hite	116th Pennsylvania Volunteer Infantry Regiment	Pennsylvania
George Hite	6th Pennsylvania Reserve Inf Regt (35th Volunteers)	Pennsylvania
George Hite	6th Pennsylvania Hvy Arty Regiment (212th Vols)	Pennsylvania
George Hite	136th Pennsylvania Volunteer Infantry Regiment	Pennsylvania
George W. Hite	35th Indiana Volunteer Infantry Regiment	Indiana
George W. Hite	114th Ohio Volunteer Infantry Regiment	Ohio
George W. Hite	120th Ohio Volunteer Infantry Regiment	Ohio
George W. Hite	48th Ohio Infantry Battalion	Ohio
George W. Hite	208th Pennsylvania Volunteer Infantry Regiment	Pennsylvania
George W. Hite	210th Pennsylvania Volunteer Infantry Regiment	Pennsylvania
George W. Hite	1st Independent Battery, Wisconsin Light Artillery	Wisconsin
Harvey H. Hite	84th Pennsylvania Volunteer Infantry Regiment	Pennsylvania
Harvey Hite	60th Ohio Volunteer Infantry Regiment	Ohio
Harvey T. Hite	54th Ohio Volunteer Infantry Regiment	Ohio
Henry H. Hite	126th Ohio Volunteer Infantry Regiment	Ohio
Henry Hite	7th Indiana Volunteer Infantry Regiment	Indiana

Henry Hite	151st Ohio National Guard Regiment	Ohio
Henry Hite	31st Ohio Volunteer Infantry Regiment	Ohio
Henry Hite	12th Pennsylvania Cavalry Regiment (113th Vols)	Pennsylvania
Henry Hite	155th Pennsylvania Volunteer Infantry Regiment	Pennsylvania
Henry Hite	98th Pennsylvania Volunteer Infantry Regiment	Pennsylvania
Henry J. Hite	3rd Pennsylvania Vol Inf Regiment (3 months, 1961)	Pennsylvania
Henry M. Hite	8th Maryland Infantry Regiment	Maryland
Hezekiah Hite	54th Pennsylvania Volunteer Infantry Regiment	Pennsylvania
Jacob A. Hite	101st Pennsylvania Volunteer Infantry Regiment	Pennsylvania
Jacob A. Hite	171st Penn Vol Inf Regiment (Drafted Militia)	Pennsylvania
Jacob H. Hite	18th Indiana Volunteer Infantry Regiment	Indiana
Jacob Hite	28th Iowa Infantry Regiment	Iowa
Jacob Hite	2nd Maryland Infantry, Potomac Home Brigade	Maryland
Jacob Hite	51st Ohio Volunteer Infantry Regiment	Ohio
Jacob Hite	72nd Pennsylvania Volunteer Infantry Regiment	Pennsylvania
Jacob Hite	5th Pennsylvania Cav Regiment (65th Volunteers)	Pennsylvania
Jacob Hite	3rd Pennsylvania Cavalry Regiment (Provisional)	Pennsylvania
Jacob Hite	18th Pennsylvania Cav Regiment (163rd Volunteers)	Pennsylvania
Jacob W. Hite	18th Indiana Volunteer Infantry Regiment	Indiana
James A. Hite	Webster County Regiment, Missouri Home Guard	Missouri
James D. Hite	12th Illinois Volunteer Infantry Regiment	Illinois
James F. Hite	12th Illinois Volunteer Infantry Regiment	Illinois
James Hite	8th Illinois Volunteer Infantry Regiment	Illinois
James Hite	15th Kentucky Infantry Regiment	Kentucky
James Hite	31st Ohio Volunteer Infantry Regiment	Ohio
James Hite	23rd Ohio Volunteer Infantry Regiment	Ohio
James Hite	192nd Pennsylvania Volunteer Infantry Regiment	Pennsylvania
James J. Hite	12th Illinois Volunteer Infantry Regiment	Illinois
James J. Hite	23rd Indiana Volunteer Infantry Regiment	Indiana
James J. Hite	34th Indiana Volunteer Infantry Regiment	Indiana
James L. Hite	34th Iowa Volunteer Infantry Regiment	Iowa

APPENDIX C

James N. Hite	4th Iowa Volunteer Cavalry Regiment	Iowa
James O.K. Hite	125th Indiana Volunteer Infantry Regiment	Indiana
James R. Hite	155th Illinois Volunteer Infantry Regiment	Illinois
James S. Hite	8th Illinois Volunteer Infantry Regiment	Illinois
James T. Hite	12th Illinois Volunteer Infantry Regiment	Illinois
James T. Hite	154th Ohio Infantry Regiment (National Guard)	Ohio
John A. Hite	61st Illinois Volunteer Infantry Regiment	Illinois
John A. Hite	8th Illinois Vol Infantry Regiment (3 months, 1861)	Illinois
John C. Hite	20th Illinois Volunteer Infantry Regiment	Illinois
John F. Hite	8th Maryland Volunteer Infantry Regiment	Maryland
John H. Hite	54th Pennsylvania Volunteer Infantry Regiment	Pennsylvania
John Hite	28th Illinois Volunteer Infantry Regiment	Illinois
John Hite	12th Indiana Volunteer Infantry Regiment	Indiana
John Hite	18th Indiana Volunteer Infantry Regiment	Indiana
John Hite	1st Missouri Volunteer Cavalry Regiment	Missouri
John Hite	2nd Missouri State Militia Cavalry Regiment	Missouri
John Hite	5th Pennsylvania Cav Regiment (65th Volunteers)	Pennsylvania
John Hite	3rd Pennsylvania Heavy Artillery Regiment	Pennsylvania
John Hite	184th Pennsylvania Volunteer Infantry Regiment	Pennsylvania
John Hite	9th Pennsylvania Cav Regiment (92nd Volunteers)	Pennsylvania
John Hite	102th Pennsylvania Volunteer Infantry Regiment	Pennsylvania
John Hite	205th Pennsylvania Volunteer Infantry Regiment	Pennsylvania
John Hite	188th Pennsylvania Volunteer Infantry Regiment	Pennsylvania
John M. Hite	72nd Ohio Volunteer Infantry Regiment	Ohio
John M. Hite	8th Ohio Volunteer Infantry Regiment	Ohio
John M. Hite	8th Ohio Volunteer Infantry Regiment	Ohio
Josiah K. Hite	136th Pennsylvania Volunteer Infantry Regiment	Pennsylvania
Josiah M. Hite	19th Pennsylvania Cav Regiment (180th Volunteers)	Pennsylvania
Martin K. Hite	72nd Ohio Volunteer Infantry Regiment	Ohio
Peasen D. Hite	12th West Virginia Volunteer Infantry Regiment	West Virginia
Stacy M. Hite	31st Ohio Infantry Regiment	Ohio

Thomas M. Hite	102nd Illinois Infantry Regiment	Illinois
Thomas M. Hite	5th Kentucky Volunteer Infantry Regiment	Kentucky
Thomas M. Hite	5th Pennsylvania Reserve Infantry (34th Volunteers)	Pennsylvania
William B. Hite	1st West Virginia Cavalry Regiment	West Virginia

Note: This tally was compiled from a 2014 search of the Ancestry.com database. Fragmentary records make it impossible to determine some soldiers' identities definitively. Some Union soldiers are probably double-counted, and many are missing from this tally. The Union roster is clearly incomplete, since no soldiers with last names starting with I, N, O, or R are listed, and only one soldier's name appears beginning with M, S, and W. There are most likely more individuals who served, especially for the South, for whom no records exist.

One citizen soldier of note who is omitted from this roster is Private Samuel C. Hite, born December 31, 1835, in Puzzletown, Blair County, Pennsylvania. He enlisted in Company A, 55th Pennsylvania Volunteer Infantry Regiment, on February 23, 1864, in Johnstown, Cambria County, and died of diarrhea on July 16, 1864, in Andersonville Prison, Macon County, Georgia. Private Hite was one of four sons of Conrad Hite (1793–1875) and Margaret Helm (1795–1881). (See page 22 for more on his family.)

Samuel C. Hite
55th Pennsylvania Volunteer Infantry
Andersonville Prison, Georgia

APPENDIX C

This branch of the Hite family originated about fifty kilometers southwest of Major Hite's forebears' ancestral home. No doubt many other Hites who fought for the North came from this and other Hite branches whose members had settled north of the Mason-Dixon Line, although clearly some of Jost's descendants who had moved westward and no longer lived in slave-centered environments also supported the Union cause.

Samuel's older brother John Hite died on April 2, 1864, during the siege of Petersburg and was buried near the Union army IX Corps field hospital at Meade Station. John was born June 26, 1830, and enlisted August 27, 1864, as a private in Company I, 205th Pennsylvania Infantry (he is included in the roster and is listed on p. 114). Both were married and left families; they also had two other brothers who served and survived the war.

Another John Hite (also included in the roster on p. 114), served in the 5th Pennsylvania Cavalry Regiment and was born December 6, 1835. He enlisted in Philadelphia as a private in Company D, 5th Pennsylvania Cavalry (also known as "Cameron's Dragoons," or the 65th Pennsylvania Regiment), on July 30, 1861, was promoted to corporal on January 19, 1862, and died on March 16, 1864, while the regiment was serving in the Army of the James at Bermuda Hundred. The regiment suffered huge casualties, including many deaths because of disease, while campaigning near the Great Dismal Swamp. Hite is buried in Webster Cemetery, Huntersville, Lycoming County, Pennsylvania.

APPENDIX D

Major Hite's Grandsons
(CSA) served in CSA; GG Great-Grandson

B y first wife **Eleanor "Nelly" Conway Madison (1760–1802):**

1) **James Madison Hite (1788–1791)** ~ died at three years
2) **Eleanor "Nelly" Conway Hite (1789–1830) & Dr. Cornelius Elijah Baldwin Jr. (1790–1828)**
    - Eleanor Conway Baldwin (1810–1849) & Edward Jaquelin Davison (1805–1848)
    GG (CSA) Pvt. William Smith Davison, Esq. (1845–1905)   Co D, 23rd VA Cav Regt ~ lost arm at Fishers Hill

    Dr. Isaac Hite Baldwin (1813–1882) ~ too old for CW duty; army surgeon during Seminole Wars
    - James Madison Baldwin (1821–1876) ~ Probably too old for field duty
    (CSA) Dr. Robert Stuart Baldwin Sr. (1824–1898) ~ surgeon

3) **James Madison Hite Sr. (1793–1860) & Caroline Matilda Irvine (1798–1877)**
   \• Isaac Irvine Hite Sr. (1820–1876) & Susan Burwell Meade (1821–1852) ~ too old
      + **GG** (CSA) Pvt. Isaac Irvine Hite Jr. (1841–1861),   Co D, 1st VA Cav Regt
      + **GG** (CSA) Pvt. William Meade Hite (1847–1863) Carpenter's Lt Arty/27th Inf
   (CSA) Pvt. James Madison Hite Jr. (1825–1892) Co D, 1st VA Cav Regt; hired substitute

Ten children with **Ann Tunstall Maury (1782–1851):**

1) **Ann Maury Hite (1806–1833) & Phillip Croudson Williams II (1811–1862)**
   Dr. Phillip Croudson Williams III (1828–1896) ~ no record of service
2) **Isaac Fontaine Hite Sr. 1807–1890 & Maria Louisa "Neddy" Davison (1808–1889)**
   Gabriel Jacob Hite (1830–1868) ~ no record of service
   Isaac Hite Jr. (1834–1835) ~ died in infancy
   Edward S. Hite (1850–1854) ~ died at four years
3) **Mary Eltinge Hite (1808–1866) & John Smith "Bull" Davison, Esq. (1802–1874)**
   John Smith Davison (1837–1913) ~ no record of service

   Walker Maury Davison (1841–1855) ~ died before the war
   Dr. William Armstrong Davison (1848–1907) ~ too young
   Alexander MacDonald Davison Jr. (1859–1880) ~ too young

4) **Rebecca Grymes Hite (1810–1851) & Rev John Lodor (1796–1864)**
   John Shepherd Lodor (1837—?) ***Possibly*** joined 14th VA Inf Regt; may have enlisted in the US Army postwar (which would make him a real "black sheep.")

APPENDIX D

5) **Dr. Walker Maury Hite Sr. & (1811–1890) & Mary Eleanor Williams (1816–1890)**
   (CSA) Pvt. Isaac Williams Hite (1837–1930)   Co H, 19th; 62nd Inf Regt
   Edmund Hite (1839—?) - probably died in infancy
   + (CSA) Pvt. Thornton Fontaine "Frank" Hite (1839–1861)   Co F, 1st VA Cav
   + (CSA) Pvt. George Smith Hite (1847–1862)   Co H, 19th VA Inf
   (CSA) Pvt. Walker Maury Hite (1848–1880)   Amherst-Nelson Light Arty
   John James Williams Hite (1857–1900) - too young

6) **Sarah Clark Macon Hite (1812–1896) & Judge Mark Bird (1810–1883)**
   (CSA) Sgt. Mark Bird Jr. (1836–1903)   Co F, 10th VA Inf
   (CSA) Pvt. Isaac Hite Bird (1845–1892)   Co C, 7th VA Cav
   William Maury Bird (1847–1934) - no information
   George Hite Bird (1848–1923) - probably too young
   Eltinge Fontaine Bird (1853–1933) - too young
   Cornelius W. Bird (1858—?) - probably died before the war

7) **Penelope Elizabeth Lee Hite (1814–1838) & Raleigh Brown Green (1808–1841)**
   Died in childbirth

8) **Hugh Holmes Hite Sr. (1816–1870) & Anne Randolph Meade (1818–1860)**
   + (CSA) Pvt. Hugh Scott Hite Jr. (1839–1862)   Co A, 17th VA Inf
   (CSA) Pvt. Kidder Meade Hite (1840–1896)   Co M, 17th VA Inf
   (CSA) Pvt. Cornelius Randolph Hite (18458–1918) Co H, 19th VA Inf
   Lewis Bates Hite (1848—?) - probably died young
   Henry Walter Hite (1849–1910) - too young
   Rev. Louis Field Hite (1852–1945) - too young
   Ludwell Bolton Hite (1857–1876) - too young

Maury Grymes Hite (1858—?) - probably died young

9) **Cornelius Baldwin Hite Sr. (1816–1841) & Elizabeth Augusta Smith (1818–1900)**
(CSA) Pvt. Cornelius Baldwin Hite Jr. (1842–1943) Co F, 1st & Co D, 6th Cavs

10) **Matilda Madison Hite (1819–1853) & Dr. Alexander McDonald Davison Sr. (1813–1889)**
Donald Monroe Powell Davison (1841—?) - probably died young
Macdonald Alexander Davison (1843–1849) - died before the war
John Smith Davison (1846–1906) - No information
+ (CSA) Pvt. Cornelius Hite Davison (1848–1865)   Shelby's Iron
                                                                  Bde, MO
Alexander McDonald Davison Jr. (1859–1860) - died before the war

INDEX

Andersonville Prison, Georgia	26, 27, 115
Augusta County, Virginia	4
Baldwin, Dr. Robert Stuart	39, 118
Belle Grove Plantation	1
Belle Grove National Historical Park	1
Bird,	
- Isaac Hite	40, 120
- Mark Jr.	41, 120
Brown, John	12
Cedar Creek (Battle)	v,1
Clarke County, Virginia (creation of)	19, 20
Cost of the Civil War	50-53
Davison,	
- Cornelius Hite	30*32, 121
- William Smith (GG)	45-49, 118
Deserters	73, 74
First Families of Virginia	8. 9, 23
Fairfax, Lord Thomas	4
Fishers Hill (Battle)	47
Frederick County, Virginia	4, 19, 20

Harpers Ferry	12
Great Indian Trail	3
Hite,	
- Conrad	26, 115
- Cornelius Baldwin "Nealy" Jr.	36, 37, 120
- Cornelius Randolph	38, 120
- Christopher	27
- David Christian	69, 70
- David Henry (Doctor)	26
- George Smith	32, 120
- Hugh Holmes Sr.	17, 33, 120
- Hugh Holmes "Scott" Jr.	33, 34, 120
- Isaac Jr. (Major)	1, 118
- Isaac Fontaine Sr.	17, 119
- Isaac Irvine Jr. (GG)	35, 119
- Isaac Williams	44, 119
- James Madison Sr.	19, 118
- James Madison Jr.	44, 119
- Johann (John) Heyt	26, 115
- John (Colonel)	4
- John	27, 117
- John Pendleton	75-77
- Jost	2, 4
- Kidder Meade	45, 120
- Robert Woodson "Wood"	51
- Samuel C.	26, 115
- Thornton Fontaine "Frank"	34, 119
- Dr. Walker Maury Sr	17, 119
- Walker Maury Jr	40, 120
- William Meade (GG)	28, 36-38, 119
- William Francis (First Lieutenant)	82
James brothers	51
Jefferson, Thomas	1, 8

INDEX

Lodor, John Shepherd	119
Madison,	
- President James	5
- Eleanor "Nelly"	5, 118
Maury, Ann Tunstall	5, 17, 119
National Park Service	1
Nat Turner's Rebellion	12
Orange County	4
Payne, Dolley Todd	5
Pennypacker Mills	3
Shenandoah County	16, 20
Shenandoah Valley	
- Civil War in	1, 25, 52, 53
- Pre-War Conditions	18-22
- Settlement	2-4
Slavery	11-17
Springdale	3, 4
Toms Brook (cavalry battle)	47
Winchester, Virginia	
- Town	19,-21
- Battles	47, 69
Valley Pike	20

Made in the USA
Middletown, DE
05 June 2016